PERGAMON INSTITUTE OF ENGLISH (OXFORD)

Council Of Europe Modern Languages Project

WAYSTAGE ENGLISH

Other Titles in the Series

The Council of Europe was established by ten nations on 5 May 1949, since when its membership has progressively increased to twenty-one. Its aim is "to achieve a greater unity between its Members for the purpose of safeguarding and realising the ideals and principles which are their common heritage and facilitating their economic and social progress". This aim is pursued by discussion of questions of common concern and by agreements and common action in economic, social, cultural, scientific, legal and administrative matters.

The Council for Cultural Cooperation was set up by the Committee of Ministers of the Council of Europe on 1 January 1962 to draw up proposals for the cultural policy of the Council of Europe, to coordinate and give effect to the overall cultural programme of the organisation and to allocate the resources of the Cultural Fund. All the member governments of the Council of Europe, together with the Holy See and Finland which have acceded to the European Cultural Convention, are represented on the Council for Cultural Cooperation.

The aim of the work carried out by the Council for Cultural Cooperation in the area of modern language learning is to encourage the development of *understanding, cooperation* and *mobility* among Europeans by improving and broadening the learning of *modern languages* by all sections of the population. This aim will be pursued

- by making generally available the basic tools for the systematic planning, construction and conduct of learning programmes geared to the needs and motivations of the learners and to the changing requirements of society;
- by helping to prepare teachers to play their proper roles in such programmes,
- and by further developing a framework for close and effective international cooperation in the promotion of language learning.

For this purpose, and under the authority of the Council for Cultural Cooperation, a number of studies have been prepared, some of which are being published in this Council of European Modern Language Series. However, the opinions expressed in the studies written in this framework are not to be regarded as reflecting the policy of any government, of the Committee of Ministers or the Secretary General of the Council of Europe.

Applications for reproduction and translation should be addressed to the Director of Education, Culture and Sport, Council of Europe, Strasbourg (France).

WAYSTAGE ENGLISH

An intermediary objective below Threshold
Level in a European unit/credit system
of modern language learning by adults

Prepared for the

COUNCIL OF EUROPE

by

J A VAN EK
University of Groningen

and

L G ALEXANDER
in association with

M A FITZPATRICK
Deutscher Volkhochschul-Verband

Published for and on behalf of the
COUNCIL OF EUROPE
by

PERGAMON PRESS
OXFORD · NEW YORK · TORONTO · SYDNEY · PARIS · FRANKFURT

U.K.	Pergamon Press Ltd., Headington Hill Hall, Oxford OX3 OBW, England
U.S.A.	Pergamon Press Inc., Maxwell House, Fairview Park, Elmsford, New York 10523, U.S.A.
CANADA	Pergamon of Canada, Suite 104, 150 Consumers Road, Willowdale, Ontario M2J 1P9, Canada
AUSTRALIA	Pergamon Press (Aust.) Pty. Ltd., P.O. Box 544, Potts Point, N.S.W. 2011, Australia
FRANCE	Pergamon Press SARL, 24 rue des Ecoles, 75240 Paris, Cedex 05, France
FEDERAL REPUBLIC OF GERMANY	Pergamon Press GmbH, 6242 Kronberg-Taunus, Pferdstrasse 1, Federal Republic of Germany

First edition 1977

This edition 1980

British Library Cataloguing in Publication Data

Ek, Jan Ate van
Waystage English. – (Pergamon Institute of English
(Oxford). Council of Europe language learning series).
1. English language – Study and teaching –
Foreign students 2. English language – Study
and teaching – Europe
I. Title II. Alexander, L G III. Fitzpatrick, M A
482'.2'40715   PE1128.A2   79-42966

ISBN 0-08-024590-0 Flexicover

Printed and bound in Great Britain by
William Clowes (Beccles) Limited, Beccles and London

CONTENTS

PREFACE TO THIS EDITION

Following the publication of *The Threshold Level* in 1975, it became clear that language teachers in Europe – and indeed further afield – welcomed the approach it incorporated and the model for the explicit statement of communicative objectives which it presented. On the other hand, as had been expected, it also became clear that although it had been devised as the lowest level of general language proficiency to be recognized in a system of objectives (because unless the language we have learnt is capable of covering a reasonably full range of social needs we cannot speak of a general level at all) such expressions as 'lowest level' and 'minimal means' could be very misleading. For adults starting to learn English from the very start, it was a long and demanding task to reach the goal of being able to move relatively freely in another society. Moreover, since in most European countries English is now taught to most if not all pupils in secondary schools, true adult beginners would often be the middle aged, or the educationally underprivileged. One of the basic principles of the Modern Languages Project has been that educational provision should be appropriate to the needs, motivations, characteristics and resources of the learner. For the learner who has no record of academic success, no established study ability and limited time and energy at his disposal, Threshold Level is not a 'minimal' but an ambitious, far-off objective. Remember that we are thinking not just of a knowledge of the elements, but the ability to put them into use in the hurly-burly of daily life.

It is an important educational objective to bring the less successful school leavers back into the educational process by giving them the experience of success, following limited short-term goals which are in themselves both useful and within the reach of the great majority. Swedish experience with the multi-media series *Start* had demonstrated the value of radio and television in reaching this audience. In 1977, under the aegis of the Council of Europe, with strong encouragement and support from the German *Bundesministerium für Bildung und Wissenschaft* and its Austrian counterpart, a powerful group of interests were brought together to plan a large-scale multi-media English course for Germany, Switzerland and Austria. The television programmes were to be co-produced by *Norddeutscher Rundfunk, Bayrischer Rundfunk* and *BBC English by Radio and Television.* Course books were planned for learners at home and those studying within the framework of the *Deutscher Volkshochschul-Verband* (VHS), which not only provided a network of classes, but also the programme co-ordinator and an intensive programme of teacher training, as well as tests at the end of each year within the framework of the certification programme of the *Internationale Zertifikatskommission.* The associated Adolf-Grimme-Institut undertook the task of monitoring and evaluating the programme. This undertaking, now brought to fruition, represents an extraordinary achievement and a long step forward in inter-institutional and international co-operation. The specific contribution of the Council of Europe was to commission a course design, produced by the distinguished British designer of EFL courses, L G Alexander.

In this context a developed objective for a one-year multi-media course was urgently needed, since it was agreed that the VHS *Zertifikat* was, on average, a three-year objective and T-level a two-year objective. In principle, many different routes to T-level could be followed: half the functional-notional areas could be covered; structural skills could be developed in the first year and applicational skills in the

vii

second; in fact Dr van Ek and Mr Alexander, working in consultation with Mr Fitzpatrick as course co-ordinator, closely concerned with the development of the corresponding *Grundbaustein* in the VHS system, followed what most people will probably recognize to be the most satisfactory principle, that of 'recycling' discussed by Wilkins in his 1973 paper.* As a result, there is as wide a coverage and as great a simplicity of means as can be derived from within the T-level specification. Accordingly, whilst *Waystage* is given the status only of one of a number of possible intermediate objectives on the way to T-level (and we should not favour a 'minimalism' which saw this first objective as a terminal goal for the mass of learners) it has in fact a coherence and breadth which make it a worthwhile objective in its own right.

J L M Trim
London, 1980

---

* Wilkins, D A 'The linguistic and situational content of the common core in a unit/credit system', in Systems Development in Adult Language Learning, Council of Europe, Strasbourg, 1973 / Pergamon Press, Oxford, 1980.

1. INTRODUCTION

1. General introduction

In 1975 the Council of Europe issued a document under the title of *The Threshold Level in a European unit/credit system for modern language learning by adults*. This was followed a year later by *The Threshold Level for modern-language learning in schools*.

The *Threshold Level* is an attempt to state as explicitly as possible what the learners will have to be able to do in a foreign language if they wish:

> 'to be able to cope, linguistically speaking, in temporary contacts with foreign language speakers in everyday situations, whether as visitors to the foreign country or with visitors to their own country, and to establish and maintain social contacts'.

In the European unit/credit system this objective is presented as the lowest level of general foreign language ability. It is assumed that the objective as defined represents the minimum that is required in order to function adequately in those communication situations in which the members of the target group, 'general beginners', are most likely to need the ability to use a foreign language. In the present state of our knowledge this can be no more than an assumption. It would appear, however, that this assumption is supported on a sufficiently large scale to justify its adoption as a working basis for the planning of modern language programmes. This means, in effect, that the Threshold Level is offered as the lowest terminal objective in these programmes and that the learners must be given every encouragement not to discontinue their studies before they have reached at least this objective. Yet, reaching the *Threshold Level* is by no means an undemanding task. With its emphasis on the ability to use the foreign language functionally in a large number of situations, with all the structural variety required for this and its vocabulary content of 1100–1500 items it will demand a sustained learning effort and at least some 120–200 hours of instruction. It is obvious that in the eyes of many learners – especially of those with little experience of educational success – such a learning task will look very formidable indeed.

Since it is the professed aim of the unit/credit scheme not only to provide opportunities for language learning but also to induce people to use these opportunities, it will be necessary to structure this learning task in such a way that it may be presented to the learner as a series of manageable steps rather than as one single daunting whole. Some sort of unit organization within the *Threshold Level* would therefore seem to be required. However, until more experience has been gained in the planning of *Threshold Level* courses, it would be premature to propose such a compartmentalization of the syllabus.

It was decided instead to begin by defining one intermediary objective, roughly halfway between zero and the *Threshold Level*. The definition of such an objective would serve at least two useful purposes. It would enable the designers to try out what they considered to be fundamental structuring principles, principles which might later on be applied in establishing a more ambitious unit structure. Secondly, it would provide an objective which many learners might be expected to be able to teach within a comparatively short period. It was felt that such a short-term objective, if given proper recognition, would be a powerful tool in promoting the motivation of

1

particularly those learners who had not previously engaged in courses of longer duration. This objective was called *Waystage*. The term indicates that, within the unit/credit system, this objective is not presented as a terminal objective, but rather as an articulation point for courses leading up to *Threshold Level*. Learners whose successful completion of the first half of such courses is given due recognition will be encouraged, it is assumed, to undertake the additional learning effort which is needed to take them to full *Threshold Level*. In the system, the *Threshold Level* is presented as the lowest objective for general foreign language ability. *Waystage*, however, is not given the status of an objective 'in its own right'. It is presented as a possible objective for the first half of courses leading up to *Threshold Level*. Yet, we would fail in our attempt to make *Waystage* the powerful tool for increasing motivation it is meant to be if we relied on extrinsic motivation only. After studying for a year or even longer, many learners are hardly likely to be fully satisfied with just the teacher's approval, the acquisition of some 'credits' or a similar pat-on-the-back reward. Especially adult learners will need the intrinsic motivation of realizing that their learning efforts are successful in a more meaningful way in that their ability to cope with foreign language situations is significantly increasing. Consequently, even without being offered as a terminal objective, *Waystage* will have to constitute a worthwhile level of ability in that it will enable the learners to cope at least minimally in those communication situations which may be most directly relevant to them.

Since *Waystage* is directly derived from the *Threshold Level*, a full understanding of the nature of the latter objective is necessary for a correct use of the present document. The *Threshold Level* is the first objective to be defined within the unit/credit system. It exemplifies the strict application of a model developed for the specification of all language-learning objectives within the system. This model is described in part 2 of this introduction. Part 3 gives a brief description of those features of the *Threshold Level* which are particularly relevant to the development of *Waystage*. Part 4 deals with the relations between *Threshold Level* and *Waystage* and the principles used in the derivation of the latter objective from the former. The other chapters deal with *Waystage* directly. A general description of the objective is given in Chapter II, and Chapter III contains the content-specification of *Waystage* in terms of functions, notions and their exponents (see part 2 of the introduction). The total lexical and structural content of the objective is presented in the form of lexical and structural inventories in Chapters IV and V respectively.

Waystage and *Threshold Level* specifications have profound implications for language course design and, by extension, for language teaching and learning. These implications were discussed by L G Alexander in a separate document published as an appendix to this volume.

2. The model

2.1 *Behavioural objectives*

The basic characteristic of the model used in the specification of objectives in the unit/credit system is that it serves to specify foreign language ability as *skill* rather than *knowledge*. It analyzes what the learner will have to be able to *do* in the foreign language and determines only in the second place what *language-forms* (words,

2

structures, etc) the learner will have to be able to handle in order to *do* all that has been specified. In accordance with the nature of verbal communication as a form of *behaviour* the objectives defined by means of this model are therefore basically *behavioural* objectives. To preclude misunderstanding it should perhaps be pointed out right at the beginning of our presentation that a behavioural specification of an objective by no means implies the need for a behaviouristic teaching method. The way in which the objective has been defined does not impose any particular methodology – behaviouristic or otherwise – on the teacher.

2.2 Explicitness

Objectives defined by means of our model have a high degree of explicitness. Yet, they are not explicit in an absolute sense. Language learning objectives can never be defined with absolute explicitness because language use is neither fully predictable (except perhaps in the most restricted situations) nor fully describable. Nevertheless, definitions based on our model are more explicit than most definitions of language learning objectives. This has obvious advantages in that it gives all those involved in the teaching/learning process, including the learners themselves, a clear view of just what is expected of them. The result of this should be a considerable increase of efficiency.

2.3 Functions and notions

In essence, the model is a very simple one, in that it analyzes verbal behaviour into only two components: the performance of *language functions* and the expression of, or reference to, *notions*. What people do by means of language can be described as verbally performing certain *functions*. By means of language people assert, question, command, expostulate, persuade, apologize, etc. In performing such functions people express, refer to or – to use a more general term – handle certain notions. They will, for instance, apologize for *being late*, for being late for a *party*, for being late for a party *yesterday*, etc. Other notions are less directly correlated with lexical items, eg the notion of 'possession', which may be expressed by means of a verb (have, possess, etc), but also by means of a prepositional construction (*of* + nominal group), a genitive case or a possessive pronoun.

It goes without saying that, although the above distinction between functions and notions was described in terms of *language production*, the same distinction applies to *language comprehension*. In the latter case, for instance, people recognize that an apology is being made and what the apology is being made for. This act of recognition may be described in terms of the interpretation of the exponents of language functions and the 'handling' of certain notions.

Our task, then, in defining a language-learning objective, is to determine what language functions the learners will have to be able to perform and what notions they will have to be able to handle.

2.4 Determining factors

It will be obvious that we can only perform our task if we have some insight into what may be expected to be the communication needs of the learners. This, in turn, would

3

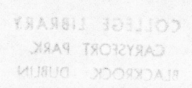

seem to depend very much on the learners themselves, on the type of contacts they may be expected to have which necessitate the use of a foreign language. The first step towards the specification of an objective is, therefore, the selection of a target group and a general characterization of the type of foreign language contacts its members may be expected to engage in. Subsequently we attempt to describe the nature of these contacts more precisely. We may determine whether the learners will be expected to have mainly (or even exclusively) *oral* contacts or *written* contacts, whether they will use the foreign language mainly (or exclusively) *receptively*, as listeners or readers, or also *productively*, as speakers or writers. In other words, we determine the *language activities* the learners are expected to engage in. We may also determine *where* they may be expected to use the foreign language. Especially for target groups with restricted (eg professional) needs this may be highly relevant. If a telephone operator is expected to use a foreign language almost exclusively in front of a switchboard, this *setting* is obviously an important factor in determining what language functions she will have to fulfil and what notions she will have to handle. Another factor is the *roles*[1] the learners may have to play. Will they have to be able to play mainly subordinate roles or will they have to command, to instruct? Apart from these *social roles* we may distinguish *psychological roles*. A 'gentle persuader's' language needs will, to a certain extent, differ from those of a 'bully', to mention two extremes. Then, of course, the *topics* the learner may be expected to deal with will have an important influence on, particularly, the notions he will have to be able to handle. It will make a lot of difference whether a learner will deal mainly with the topic of public transport, as a railway employee may do, or with the topic of health, ailments, accidents, as may be the case with a nurse. To a certain extent, we can integrate the various factors mentioned above by specifying for each topic just what the learners may be expected to *do* with regard to it. This relates language activities, settings and roles directly to the topics.

To sum up: we determine what language functions the learners will have to be able to fulfil and what notions they will have to be able to handle on the basis of:

- a general characterization of the type of language contacts which, as members of a certain target group they will engage in;
- the language activities they will engage in;
- the settings in which they will use the foreign language;
- the roles (social and psychological) they will play;
- the topics they will deal with;
- what they will be expected to do with regard to each topic.

It goes without saying that, except in extreme cases, our decisions with regard to each component will only be based on estimates. We cannot possibly predict with certainty exactly what a learner is going to do with a foreign language once he has mastered it to a certain degree. We can, however, make useful estimates and prepare the learner for those foreign language contacts he is most likely to engage in. Moreover, such is the transfer potential of linguistic ability, once the learner has been successfully prepared for certain foreign-language contacts he will find that he can also cope more or less adequately in numerous other foreign-language situations.

If the above components play an important role in determining our choice of language functions and of notions for a certain objective, they also influence – in many cases even decisively – our choice of *exponents* for the various functions and

4

notions. By exponents we mean the actual language forms by means of which the learner will fulfil each function and express each notion. It will be obvious that, for instance, the actual *language forms* the learner will be taught to use in order to fulfil the function 'asking others to do something' will depend to a large extent on the social and psychological roles he will be playing. In this respect, too, the specification is learner-orientated in that, in each decision we make, we ask ourselves what is most appropriate to a particular class of learners, what will most adequately satisfy their individual foreign language communication needs.

2.5 Common core and specific notions

It cannot be said that each of the above components is equally influential in each choice we make. This applies particularly to the component which we called 'topics'. Some parts of the specification will be more directly affected by our selection of particular topics than others. The linguistic needs for asking, inviting, apologizing – in short, for the functions – will be less stringently determined by the choice of a particular topic than those for expressing certain concrete notions. Whether the learners will need to be able to express the notion 'peanut-butter' or the notion 'airport' will depend more directly on the situations he will find himself in, particularly the topics he will deal with, than the need to refer to past, future, present or to say whether something is located before, behind, under or above something else. This is a reason for making another subdivision in our specification. We subdivide the notions into *general notions* and *specific notions*. The specific notions are those that are directly determined by our choice of individual topics, whereas the general notions are appropriate to a large variety of topics, to a large variety of situations. This generality with respect to the topics also characterizes the language functions. We can therefore group the language functions and the general notions together and refer to them as the 'common core', to distinguish them from the strictly topic-related specific notions.

We have now successively made the following subdivisions:

I.	language functions	notions	
II.	language functions	general notions	specific notions

III.	common core		
	language functions	general notions	specific notions

2.6 Adaptability

The last subdivision offers the clue to the reconciliation of the need for comprehensive learning systems and the individual requirements of a variety of sub-groups within a target population. The organization of large-scale learning systems is, on the whole, only practically viable if (potential) learners can be grouped together into large target

5

groups. All the members of such target groups will show the same general characteristics and will have the same overall language needs. Yet, the larger the target group, the greater the differences in specific needs and interests will be. In other words, a large target group will inevitably consist of a number of sub-groups whose needs and interests are largely identical but at the same time in some respects significantly different.

The distinction within the specification of an objective between a common core and a category of specific notions makes it possible to adapt an objective for a large target group to the requirements of each individual sub-group within this target group without changing its identity in any essential way. It simply means that, with perhaps certain minor reservations, the common core will be the same for all members of the overall target group but that the category of specific notions will be adapted to the needs and interests of each individual sub-group by replacing certain topics from which they have been derived by other topics and making the corresponding changes in the specific notions. Thus the overall communicative ability as specified in the objective will be common to all learners, both in level and in range, but certain sub-groups will be more competent in dealing with certain topics than other sub-groups.

3. The Threshold Level

3.1 Application of the model

The application of the model in the construction of an objective involves making a number of successive choices. As described in Chapter 2, these choices have to be made with regard to:

- target groups;
- language activities;
- settings;
- roles;
- topics;
- language functions;
- general notions;
- specific notions;
- exponents.

3.2 Target group

The target group chosen for the *Threshold Level* was that of general beginners, particularly those who would have the following characteristics:

- they would be temporary visitors to the foreign country (especially tourists);
  or
    they would have temporary contacts with foreigners in their own country;
- their contacts with foreign-language speakers would, on the whole, be of a superficial, non-professional type;
- they would primarily need only a basic level of command of the foreign language.

6

3.3 Language-activities

The *Threshold Level*, in accordance with the estimated needs of the target group, is essentially a level of oral communicative ability. It is assumed that for this target group the most important language activity is carrying on a conversation. This involves two skills: speaking and understanding. The objectives for reading and writing at *Threshold Level* are strictly limited to certain specified language acts and fall short of what might be called 'general ability'.

3.4 Settings

The members of the target group will learn the foreign language for general purposes. This means that the specification of what they will have to learn is not particularly geared to any special setting or types of setting (as might be the case in specifications for professional purposes). The learners will be expected to use their foreign language ability in such a variety of settings, ranging from a family living-room to an open-air swimming pool, from a post office or to a friend's bed-sitter, that an attempt to enumerate them can be neither very successful nor particularly useful. Those readers who would nevertheless prefer to have some guidance on this point are referred to Chapter 5 of the *Threshold Level* specification for adults[2] where some 90 settings are listed.

3.5 Roles

It would be both unrealistic and unnecessary to require that at a minimum level the learner should be able to play any other than the more neutral roles. Although we might like the learner to have the ability to play also more strongly marked roles and to use the highly informal, typical formal, condescending or self-effacing kind of language that might go with them, this is obviously something to be aimed at at higher levels than the minimum level. On the whole, the inclusion of any typically marked language forms in the *Threshold Level* specification has been avoided. Although the learners' language may consequently sound somewhat colourless, it will at least save them from committing social blunders through an inappropriate use of strongly marked language forms.

The principal social roles which, at *Threshold Level*, the learner is expected to be able to play are those of stranger/stranger and friend/friend, the psychological roles those of neutrality, equality, sympathy, antipathy.

3.6 Topics

It will be clear that in the choices made for the component 'topics' there is a stronger element of subjectivity than in the choices for the other components. On the face of it, it might even seem to be an impossible task to determine which topics general learners will be most likely to deal with in a foreign language. Yet, teaching would not be possible unless such a selection were made. Moreover, it appears that where efforts have been made to draw up lists of topics for general learners the results have, on the whole, been very similar in each case. Such lists have been made on the basis of common sense, intuition, introspection, experience. It would appear that on this basis a high degree of consensus may be reached, which will counter-balance the

7

subjectivity of the selection. The selection of topics for the *Threshold Level* would seem to correspond to most teachers' views on 'what general learners need most'. In addition, the possibility of replacing certain topics by others should be an effective guarantee against the dreaded 'strait-jacket effect'.

3.7 Functions, notions, exponents

For the full lists of language-functions, general and specific notions and (English) exponents selected for the *Threshold Level* the reader is referred to the document in which this objective is defined.

4. Waystage and Threshold Level

4.1 Principles of selection

Waystage is presented as an articulation point for courses leading up to *Threshold Level* (see Chapter 1). It follows from this that it will be aimed at the same target population (see 3.2) as the *Threshold Level*, taking into account the situations in which the members of the target population are most likely to need the ability to use the foreign language. It also follows that the content of *Waystage* must be selected from that of the *Threshold Level*.

What principles are to be applied in making this selection? The first principle is that the widest possible functional range should be achieved as early as possible. Even the most naive learners start a foreign language course with the expectation that it will enable them to *do* things in the foreign language, particularly to do those things which they feel they may want to do when in contact with foreign-language speakers. In order to sustain their motivation we shall consequently have to plan their foreign language course in such a way that they can do as many of these things as possible as early as possible. To give a simple example: rather than teaching them from the start to introduce themselves in three different ways, we would prefer them to be able to do three different things each in one way. The range of expression required for fully adequate foreign language behaviour will be reached gradually. In our example this means that we would come back to *'introducing onself'* at a later stage in order to teach the other two ways of doing it. This 'recycling' is, of course, not only a grading principle below *Threshold Level*, it applies equally above it.

The second principle of selection is the old principle of increasing complexity. The language forms chosen for the first stage will, on the whole, be the simpler ones. 'Perhaps he is ill' rather than 'He may be ill', to give one example.

The third principle is that of immediate relevance. We cannot teach everything at the same time, we cannot deal with all the topics simultaneously. A selection will therefore have to be made of those topics which are likely to appeal most directly to the learners, ie those topics which they probably feel they most urgently need to be able to talk about.

The fourth principle is that of pedagogical adequacy. The selection we make will have to form a good basis for further learning. This is to say that it will not be a list of phrase book expressions to be learned parrot-fashion but that it will have to reflect the systematic properties of the language. Although the grammar contained in it will necessarily be a very incomplete one, it will nevertheless constitute a coherent body of rules, which the learners will have to be able to use creatively in their own foreign-language behaviour.

4.2 *Waystage and Threshold Level compared*

The principles discussed in 4.1 have been applied in specifying *Waystage* as defined in the present document. The specification correlates very closely with that developed for the '*Threshold Level* for adults'. Yet there is no one-to-one correspondence between the various categories, mainly because certain categories were considered to be beyond *Waystage* and consequently omitted. Furthermore, a greater consistency in the categorization has been aimed at by rearranging certain elements. It has particularly been attempted to reduce the number of cases in which identical exponents were listed in several categories. In the *Threshold Level* various exponents occur under certain topic headings (division III) without being clearly topic-related. In the present specification such exponents have been transferred to *Division II: general notions*. An important consequence of this economy is that, even more than in the case of the *Threshold Level*, users of the specifications should be aware that the lists of words under each topic-heading in division III are incomplete in that, on the whole, all the words of more general application are to be supplied from the exponents of the language functions (division I) and the general notions (division II). In other words: in 'filling' the various topics with language material, all the material contained in divisions I and II is supposed to be constantly available in addition to whatever concrete vocabulary is listed under individual topics in division III. In order to further reduce the repetitiveness which makes the *Threshold Level* look more formidable than it actually is, it was decided to refrain from including the 'labels' for individual specific notions in the lists of division III. Since in the large majority of cases the (English) exponent and the (English) name of the specific notion to which it belongs are identical, it was felt to be sufficient merely to list the exponents under each topic assuming that users would have no difficulty in supplying the labels of corresponding specific notions themselves wherever these might be required.

Unlike the *Threshold Level*, *Waystage* does not distinguish between exponents for productive *and* receptive use (marked P in the *Threshold Level*) and exponents for receptive use alone (R). At this level the learners' ability will necessarily fall short of what is minimally required in order to cope with some adequacy with the variety of language-forms they may expect to be confronted with in ordinary communication situations. Moreover, all the elements contained in *Waystage* occur as elements for productive use at *Threshold Level*.

In the present specification certain exponents with grammatical implications are underscored thus ------, indicating that, at *Waystage*, the learners are not expected to be able to use them in structurally varied contexts but only as set phrases. After reaching *Waystage* the learners will have to 'activate' these exponents and incorporate them into their grammatical repertoire.

In the vocabulary lists of division III (topic related exponents) there is a modest amount of open-endedness. Certain items are underscored thus ++++++++, indicating that the semantico-lexical categories they stand for are to be filled in

9

accordance with the needs and interests of the various sub-classes of the target population. This may mean a fairly substantial filling in some cases and an extremely short list in others. An average of four elements would seem to be reasonable. The degree of open-endedness thus introduced reflects a compromise between (a) the need for individual scope and (b) the need for guidance and unity. In fact, the items marked + + + + + + + + occur especially in those cases where it was felt that any further specification would necessarily be highly arbitrary since it would have to be geared towards only one section of the overall target population. Items marked with dotted underlining e.g. names of the days of the week (p. 23) indicate sets with a limited number of exponents.

In the present document no indications are given as to the degree of skill (fluency, formal correctness, pronunciation etc) which will be minimally required at *Waystage*. Such requirements were dealt with in very general terms in the *Threshold Level for adults* (Chapter 12) and at the present moment no further concretization is available. What was said in the *Threshold Level* will be equally valid for *Waystage* and the reader is therefore referred to the former document. This implies, of course, that in the present author's view there is no *a priori* reason to assume that at *Waystage* the learners' performance would have to be qualitatively inferior to their degree of skill at *Threshold Level*. In other words: although at *Waystage* the learners will be able to do less than at *Threshold Level*, they will not necessarily do this less well!

References

[1] Richterich, R (1972) *A model for the definition of language needs of adults learning a modern language* Council of Europe, Strasbourg. Now published by Pergamon Press, Oxford (1980).

[2] van Ek, J A (1975) *Systems development in adult language learning: the Threshold Level* Council of Europe, Strasbourg. Now published by Pergamon Press, Oxford (1980).

2. Waystage: Characterization

1. At *Waystage* the learners will have completed the first stage of a two-stage learning process ultimately resulting in a basic general foreign language ability (*Threshold Level*).

2. At *Waystage* the learners will already have the ability to fulfil the most essential language functions in a simple way and to cope, linguistically speaking, in a restricted number of foreign-language situations, especially those in which the use of the foreign language is likely to be found essential for the satisfaction of the most urgent communication needs.

3. *Waystage*, like *Threshold Level*, is an objective for those learners who would be temporary visitors to a foreign-language country or have temporary contacts with foreign-language speakers in their own country, and who would use the foreign language particularly orally and for general, non-professional purposes.

4. Although *Waystage* is a basis for achieving general foreign language ability it particularly favours the following topic areas:

   1. Personal identification
   2. House and home
   3. Free time, entertainment
   4. Travel
   5. Health and welfare
   6. Shopping
   7. Food and drink
   8. Services
   9. Places
   10. Language
   11. Weather
   12. Public notices.

5. At *Waystage* the learners will be able to fulfil the following language functions:

1. Imparting and seeking factual information

1.1 identifying
1.2 reporting (including describing and narrating)
1.3 correcting
1.4 asking.

2. Expressing and finding out intellectual attitudes

2.1 expressing agreement and disagreement
2.2 denying something
2.3 expressing that one knows or does not know something or someone
2.4 inquiring whether someone knows or does not know something or someone
2.5 accepting an offer or invitation
2.6 declining an offer or invitation

2.7   expressing ability and inability
2.8   inquiring about ability and inability
2.9   expressing how certain or uncertain one is of something
2.10 expressing one is/is not obliged to do something
2.11 inquiring whether one is obliged to do something
2.12 seeking and giving permission to do something
2.13 stating that permission is withheld.

3. Expressing and finding out emotional attitudes

3.1   expressing pleasure, liking
3.2   expressing displeasure, dislike
3.3   inquiring about liking, dislike
3.4   expressing satisfaction
3.5   expressing dissatisfaction
3.6   expressing disappointment
3.7   expressing preference
3.8   expressing gratitude
3.9   expressing intention
3.10 inquiring about intention
3.11 expressing want, desire
3.12 inquiring about want, desire.

4. Expressing moral attitudes

4.1   apologizing
4.2   granting forgiveness
4.3   expressing approval
4.4   expressing appreciation
4.5   expressing regret
4.6   expressing indifference.

5. Getting things done (suasion)

5.1   requesting others to do something
5.2   warning others to take care or to refrain from doing something
5.3   instructing or directing others to do something
5.4   offering assistance
5.5   requesting assistance
5.6   making suggestions.

6. Socializing

6.1   greeting people
6.2   when meeting people
6.3   when introducing people and when being introduced
6.4   when taking leave
6.5   attracting attention
6.6   proposing a toast.

6. At *Waystage* the learners will be able to do at least the following things* with regard to each topic area:

1. Personal identification

Say who they are, spell their name, state their address, give their telephone number, say when and where they were born, state their age, sex, say whether they are married or not, state their nationality, say where they are from, what they do for a living, describe their family, state their religion, if any; obtain similar information from others.

2. House and home

Describe a house or flat and the room in it, refer to and inquire about furniture and bedclothes, services and amenities, describe regions, particularly the one where they themselves live.

3. Free time, entertainment

Say when they are free and what they do in their spare time, particularly with reference to public entertainment, sports, reading; obtain similar information from others.

4. Travel

Use means of public transport, obtain tickets, etc, refer to means of private transport, seek accommodation, book a room, inquire about meals, etc.

5. Health and welfare

Describe what is wrong to a doctor or a dentist, report accidents, say whether they feel well, are hungry, tired, etc, obtain articles of personal hygiene, refer to medical services and emergency services.

6. Shopping

Use shopping facilities, particularly obtaining foodstuffs, clothes and household articles, discuss prices, pay for things bought.

7. Food and drink

Refer to and order various kinds of food, also in a restaurant.

8. Services

Refer to and inquire about postal services, telephone, telegraph, bank and police.

---

* These 'behavioural specifications' are to be regarded as guidelines, rather than exhaustive descriptions. In fact, the possibilities of relating the ability specified under 'language functions' and 'general notions' to the various topic areas are so numerous that an exhaustive description, even at this level, would seem to be hardly feasible.

13

9. Places

Ask the way and give strangers directions.

10. Language

Say how well they speak, understand, read, write a foreign language, ask what things are called, what a word means, ask someone to speak slowly, to repeat something, ask whether something is correct, how something is pronounced.

11. Weather

Talk about various weather conditions.

12. Public notices

Understand the text of important signs.

3. Waystage: Content specification

The following abbreviations are used in the specifications:

NP   : noun phrase, ie something which, in a sentence, has a nominal function;
VP   : verb phrase, ie a verb or verbal group with objects, if any;
N   : noun;
V_{inf} : infinitive without *to*;
V_{to} : infinitive with *to*.

Division I: Language functions with exponents for English

1. Imparting and seeking factual information

1.1	*identifying*	demonstrative pronouns *(this, that, these, those)* BE + NP (1) demonstrative adjectives *(this, that, these, those)* + N + BE + NP personal pronouns (subject forms) + BE + NP declarative sentences
1.2	*reporting (including describing and narrating*	What happened?
1.3	*correcting*	same exponents as above; in addition: adverb *no* negative sentences with *not* sentences containing the negation words *never, no* (adjective), *nothing*
1.4	*asking*	interrogative sentences (yes/no questions) question word sentences with *when, where, why, what* (pronoun), *who, what* (adjective), *how,* (+far, much, long, etc)

2. Expressing and finding out intellectual attitudes

2.1	*expressing agreement and disagreement*	Yes All right declarative sentences No (adverb) negative sentences with *not*
2.2	*denying something*	No (adverb) negative sentences with *not* sentences containing the negation words *never, no* (adjective), *nothing*

15

2.3	*expressing that one knows or does not know something or someone*	I (don't) know (+noun (–group)/pronoun)
1.4	*inquiring whether someone knows or does not know something or someone*	Do you know (+noun (–group)/pronoun)
2.5	*accepting an offer or invitation*	Yes, please <u>Thank you</u>
2.6	*declining an offer or invitation*	<u>No, thank you</u>
2.7	*expressing ability and inability*	NP + can(not) + VP
2.8	*inquiring about ability or inability*	Can(not) + NP + VP
2.9	*expressing how certain/uncertain one is of something*	
	(a) positive	declarative sentences
	(b) intermediate	I think + (so (*that*–clause
	(c) weak	Perhaps . . .
	(d) negative	I don't think + (so (*that*–clause
2.10	*expressing one is/is not obliged to do something*	I (don't) have to + VP
2.11	*inquiring whether one is obliged to do something*	Do I have to + VP
2.12	*seeking and giving permission to do something*	<u>May I/Can I</u> + VP Yes All right
2.13	*stating that permission is withheld*	(Please) don't + VP No (adverb)

3. Expressing and finding out emotional attitudes

3.1	*expressing pleasure, liking*	This/that is (very) nice I like + noun (–group)/pronoun (very much)
3.2	*expressing displeasure, dislike*	He/she/this/that is not (very) nice I don't like + noun (–group)/pronoun
3.3	*inquiring about liking /dislike*	Do you like + noun (–group)/pronoun
3.4	*expressing satisfaction*	This/that is very good/nice

16

3.5	*expressing dissatisfaction*	I don't like this/that
3.6	*expressing disappointment*	What a pity
3.7	*expressing preference (general/immediate)*	I('d) prefer + noun (–group)/pronoun I('d) like + noun (–group)/pronoun
3.8	*expressing gratitude*	Thank you (very much)
3.9	*expressing intention*	I'm going + V_{to}
3.10	*inquiring about intention*	Are you going + V_{to}
3.11	*expressing want, desire*	I'd like + { noun (–group)/pronoun (, please) { V_{to} May I have + noun (–group)/pronoun (, please) I want + { noun (–group)/pronoun { V_{to}
3.12	*inquiring about want, desire*	Would you like + { noun (–group)/pronoun { V_{to} Do you want + { noun (–group)/pronoun { V_{to}

4. Expressing moral attitudes

4.1	*apologizing*	I'm (very) sorry
4.2	*granting forgiveness*	That's all right
4.3	*expressing approval*	Good!
4.4	*expressing appreciation*	(It's) very good/nice
4.5	*expressing regret*	What a pity
4.6	*expressing indifference*	It doesn't matter

5. Getting things done (suasion)

5.1	*requesting others to do something*	Please + VP VP + please
5.2	*warning others to take care or to refrain from something*	Look out! Be careful! Don't + VP
5.3	*instructing or directing others to do something*	declarative sentences with *you* as subject imperative sentences
5.4	*offering assistance*	Can I help you?
5.5	*requesting assistance*	Can you help me, please?
5.6	*making suggestions*	Let's + VP

6. Socializing

6.1	*greeting people*	Hallo
		Good morning/afternoon/evening
6.2	*when meeting people*	Hallo?
		(How are you?)
		(I'm fine, thank you,) how are you?
6.3	*when introducing people and when being introduced*	This is . . .
		(response) How do you do?
		Hallo
6.3	*when taking leave*	Good-bye
6.5	*attracting attention*	Excuse me . . .
6.6	*proposing a toast*	Cheers!

Division II: General notions with exponents for English

1. Existential

1.1	*existence/non-existence*	There is . . .
		There is not any . . .
		Is there . . .
		to make
		She made a new dress
1.2	*presence/absence*	here
		not here
		away
1.3	*availability/non-availability*	to have } used in affirmative, negative
		to have got } and interrogative contexts
		There is . . .
		There is not any . . .
		There's no . . .
		Is there . . .
		ready
		When will it be ready?

2. Spatial

2.1	*location*	here
		there
		where?
		inside
		Come inside
		outside
		Let's go outside
		(in) the north
		He lives in the north (of England)

(in) the south
He lives in the south (of England)
(in) the west
He lives in the west (of England)
(in) the east
He lives in the east (of England)
have gone to + NP
He's gone to Paris
have been to + NP
He's been to Paris
demonstrative adjectives ⎱ this, that,
demonstrative pronouns ⎰ these, those

2.2	*relative position*	at + NP

We are going to wait at the station
He is at home
between + NP
Henley is between London and Oxford
in front of + NP
There's a tree in front of the house
beind
There's a tree behind the house
on + NP
The food was on the table
under + NP
The dog was under the table
in + NP
I live in London
in the centre (+ of + NP)
I live in the centre (of Manchester)
at the end (+ of + NP)
The hotel is at the end of the street
next to + NP
The garage is next to the hotel
inside
My car is inside
outside
My car is outside

2.3	*distance*	near + NP

We live near the railway station
far + from + NP
We don't live far from the railway station
(two miles) away
It's two miles away

2.4	*motion/immobility*	to go

Where did you go last night?
Where have you been?
to go + prepositional adjuncts of place

He went to London
He went into the house
to go home
to go out
to go away
to stop
The car stopped in front of a garage
to leave
We left the station at ten
to arrive
The train arrived at eleven
to come (+ to + NP)
He came very late
He came to our house
to get up
I have to get up at six
to sit down
I'd like to sit down now
to walk
We are going to walk to the railway station
to stay
I'm going to stay here for a week
It is not going to stay dry today
to sit
Don't sit on that table!
to stand
I had to stand in the train
to wait (+ for + NP)
We had to wait five minutes
Wait for me, please

2.5   *direction*

(to the) left
Turn left at the crossing
(to the) right
Turn right at the crossing
straight on
to + NP
This train goes to London
from + NP
He has come from London
into + NP
He went into the house
out of + NP
He came out of the house
through + NP
he went through the centre of the town
away
He walked away

20

in
Don't go in now
out
We walked out
up
Are you going up? (eg in a lift)
down
I am going down (eg in a lift)
back
We went back
to turn
Turn left at the river
to bring
Bring me some water
to send
I want to send a letter to Holland
to take
I'd like to take this with me
to put
May I put my coat here?

2.6	*origin*	from + NP
		I come from London

2.7	*arrangement*	before + NP
		A comes before B
		after + NP
		B comes after A
		first
		John came first
		last
		Peter came last
		between
		B comes between A and C

2.8	*dimension*	
2.8.1	size	big ⎫
		small ⎬ These and other adjectives to be used both attributively and predicatively, and also in the comparative degree
		high ⎬
		low ⎭
2.8.2	length	mile
		foot
		The car is thirteen ft long
		inch
		kilometre
		metre
		centimetre
		long
		This road is very long

		short
		I want a short coat
2.8.3	pressure	see II 2.8.4
2.8.4	weight	lbs
		ozs
		gram(me)s
		kilo
		heavy
		This blanket is too heavy
		light
		I want a very light blanket
2.8.5	volume	gallon
		pint
		litre
2.8.6	space	big
		small
2.8.7	temperature	warm
		hot
		cold

3. Temporal

3.1	*point of time/period*	time

What time is it?

It's ⎰ (four) o'clock
At ⎱ a quarter to/past (three)
     half past (three)
     (23) minutes to/past (three)

yesterday
today
tomorrow

this ⎰ morning
    afternoon
    evening
    week
    month
    year

last/next ⎰ week
       month
       year

tonight
last night
It's ⎱ (three) am
At ⎰ (three) pm
on (Monday)

in $\left\{\begin{array}{l}\text{July}\\ \text{spring}\\ \text{etc}\end{array}\right.$

names of the days of the week

names of the months

dates, eg (Sunday) 13 June 1976

(four days) ago

then

now

when?

spring

summer

autumn

winter

3.2	*priority*	before + NP
		present perfect
		I have not seen John yet
		I have been to Paris
		already
		I have already done it
		not yet
		He has not come yet
		yet (in questions)
		Has he come yet?

3.3	*posteriority*	after + NP
		later
		I'm going to do this later

3.4	*sequence*	first
		First we went to London
		then
		First we went to London, then we went to Paris

| 3.5 | *simultaneousness* | at the same time |

3.6   *future reference*   NP + be going to + VP

soon

next $\left\{\begin{array}{l}\text{week}\\ \text{month}\\ \text{year}\end{array}\right.$

in (four days)

tomorrow

tonight

3.7   *present reference*   present continuous

simple present

present perfect

now

today

this $\left\{\begin{array}{l}\text{morning}\\ \text{afternoon}\\ \text{year etc}\end{array}\right.$

still
He is still working

3.8	*past reference*	simple past

last { week / month / etc }

yesterday
just
I've just seen him

3.9	*reference without time focus*	simple present

Edinburgh is in Scotland

3.10	*delay*	late

The train is going to be late

3.11	*earliness*	early

You are early
There is an early train on Mondays
You came too early

3.12	*lateness*	late

too late
We were too late for the train

3.13	*length of time (duration)*	for + NP (durational nouns)

since + NP (point of time)
till + NP (point of time)
long
We had to wait a long time
short
We waited a short time
take
How long does it take?
It takes five minutes (by taxi)
year
month
week
day
hour
minute

3.14	*speed*	fast

This is a very fast car
slow
This is a slow train

3.15	*frequency*	never

sometimes
(not) often
always

24

every $\left\{\begin{array}{l}\text{Sunday}\\\text{week}\\\text{etc}\end{array}\right.$

(three) times a (week)

usually

3.16	*continuity*	present continuous
		present perfect
		I've been here for two hours
		I've lived here for two years
3.17	*intermittence*	not always
3.18	*permanence*	always
3.19	*temporariness*	for + NP (durational nouns)
		You can have my car for a week
		not always
3.20	*repetitiousness*	again
		twice
		many times
3.21	*uniqueness*	once
3.22	*commencement*	to start
		The journey started at seven
		He started to speak
		since + NP (point of time)
3.23	*cessation*	to stop
		till + NP (point of time)
3.24	*change/transition*	to change
		The weather has changed
		suddenly . . .

4. Quantitative

4.1	*number*	singular/plural (grammatical category)
		cardinal numerals up to four digits
		ordinal numerals up to two digits
		telephone numbers
		another
		May I have another cup of tea, please?
		about
		I have about £25

| 4.2 | quantity | all
any
a lot of
some
no
many
much
more
most
not any
enough
little
a little
few
a few
half } + NP |

Give me half of it
Give me the other half
Give me half a bottle
(see further division II,2.8)

$$a \begin{Bmatrix} \text{bottle} \\ \text{piece} \\ \text{cup} \\ \text{glass} \end{Bmatrix} \text{of}$$

| 4.3 | degree | very . . .
too . . .
much
a little } + comparative degree of
    adjective or adverb
almost |

5. Qualitative

5.1	Physical
5.1.1	shape	round square
5.1.2	dimension	see II.2.8
5.1.3	moisture, humidity	dry wet to dry
5.1.4	visibility, sight	NP + can(not) see + NP to look (+ at + NP) *Don't look now!* *Look at his new car* dark *It is too dark here* light *It's light at five am in summer*

26

5.1.5	audibility, hearing	NP + can(not) hear + NP
		to listen (+ to + NP)
		Listen to me please
		Listen, it is raining
		loud
		The music is too loud
		noise
		There is too much noise here
5.1.6	taste	nice
		This meat is (not) very nice
5.1.7	texture	soft
		I want a soft pillow
		hard
		This pillow is too hard
		strong
		This is very strong plastic
5.1.8	colour	blue
		black
		brown
		green
		grey
		orange
		red
		white
		yellow
		light
		I want a light colour
		dark
		I want a dark colour
		colour
		That is a nice colour
5.1.9	age	I am (23)
		How old are you (is he, she, etc)?
		old
		I am too old for this
		young
		He is very young
		year
		This house is (150) years old
		years old
		This house is (150) years old
		adult
		Adults 50p, children 20p
		child
		new
		We have got a new car

27

5.1.10	physical condition	ill
		Are you ill?
		well
		I am very well
		all right
		He/His car is all right now
		dead
		The dog is dead
		to break
		He has broken his leg
		to cut
		I have cut my hand
5.1.11	accessibility	open
		The door is open
		closed
		The door is closed
5.1.12	cleanness	clean
		This skirt is not clean
		to clean
		to wash

5.1.13 material

plastic
nylon ⎫
cotton ⎬ used attributively and as head of noun group
paper ⎭
wool used as head of noun group

5.1.14	fullness	full
		empty
		to fill

5.2 *Evaluative*

5.2.1	value, price	How much
		How much are these shoes?
		to be
		How much are these shoes?
		expensive
		cheap
5.2.2	quality	good
		bad
		better
		best
		well
		He cannot write English very well
5.2.3	acceptability	That's all right
5.2.4	adequacy/ inadequacy	(It's) all right
		(It's) enough/not enough

5.2.5	correctness/ incorrectness	right *Is that the right word?* better *Your English is better now* wrong
5.2.6	capacity/ incapacity	NP + can(not) + VP
5.2.7	importance/ unimportance	(not) important
5.2.8	abnormality	strange
5.2.9	facility/difficulty	easy difficult

6. Mental

6.1	*reflection*	(see also Division I) to know to think *I think so* *I think that you are ill* to hope *I hope that you can help me*
6.2.	*expression*	(see also Division I) to speak *Can you speak French?* to write *I want to write a letter* to talk *We talked for a long time* to say *How do you say that in English?* to tell *Tell me about your work* to ask *May I ask a question?* question *May I ask a question?* to thank

7. Relational

7.1	*Spatial relations*	See II.2.2, II.2.3, II.2.5, II.2.6, II.2.7.
7.2	*Temporal relations*	See II.3.2–II.3.12
7.3	*Action/event relations*	
7.3.1	agency	agent as subject

7.3.2	objective (including factitive)	objective as object *John opened* **the door** objective as subject **The door** *is open* factitive as object *She made a* **new dress**
7.3.3	dative	dative as indirect object *He gave* **me** *a book* dative in *to*-adjunct *He gave the ticket* **to my brother**
7.3.4	instrumental	instrumental in *with*–adjunct *You can open the door* **with this key**
7.3.5	benefactive	benefactive in *for*–adjunct *I have bought this* **for my wife**
7.3.6	place	See II.2
7.3.7	time	See II.3
7.3.8	manner, means	well badly slowly quickly How? *How can I do it?*
7.4	*Contrastive relations*	
7.4.1	equality/inequality	(not) the same (thing) different (+ from + NP) other *Give me the other book* another *Give me another (=different) book* the same as . . .
7.4.2	correspondence/ contrast	(not) the same (thing) different comparative degree of adjective + *than John is older than his brother*
7.5	*Possessive relations*	
7.5.1	ownership, possession	possessive adjectives (*my, your*, etc) possessive pronouns (*mine, yours*, etc) as complement *This is mine* genitive singular of personal nouns *of*–adjuncts *with*–adjuncts *Did you see a man with a big suitcase?* *without*–adjuncts

Don't go there without your passport
to have (got)
I have (got) a small car
to get (= to receive)
I got a nice present from him
to give
I gave him a nice present
to keep
May I keep this?

7.6 *Logical relations*

7.6.1 conjunction
and
but
I want a new car, but I have not got any money
too
John is going to come too
pair
I want to buy a pair of shoes

7.6.2 disjunction
or

7.6.3 inclusion/exclusion
with + NP
We are going to take John with us
without + NP
We cannot go without you

7.6.4 cause
Why . . .?
because + sub-clause

7.6.5 effect
then . . .
so . . .

7.6.6 reason
Why . . .?
because + sub-clause

7.6.7 purpose
to + V_{inf}
He came to help me

7.6.8 focussing
about + NP
He talked about his work
only
Milk? Only a little, please

8. **Deixis***

A. **definite**

(a) non-anaphoric:
   personal pronouns (subject forms and object forms)
   possessive adjectives (*my, your, their* etc)
   possessive pronouns (*mine, yours, theirs,* etc) as complement

31

This is mine
demonstrative adjectives (attributive *this*, *these*, *that*, *those*)
definite article *the*
interrogative pronouns (independent) *who*, *whose*, *what*, *which*
interrogative adjective (attributive) *whose*, *what*, *which*

(b) anaphoric:
personal pronouns (subject forms and object forms)
possessive adjectives
possessive pronouns as complement
You take it; it's yours
demonstrative adjectives
demonstrative pronouns
definite article *the*
propword *one* (as in: *May I have the red one, please?*)
adverbs
  here
  there
  now
  then
  so (as in: *He wanted to leave, but he did not say so*)

B. indefinite

indefinite article *a, an*
indefinite pronouns:
  nothing
  something
  anything
  all (as in: *They all went home; I want all of it*)
  it (as in: *It's raining*)
adverbs:
  never
  sometimes
  always
indefinite semi-deictics:
  people
  There are five people here
  thing
  What do you call that thing?
  to do
  What are you going to do tonight?

---

* *Deixis* is the grammatical system used for referring or identifying by means of linguistic items belonging to closed sets. Deixis may be *definite* or *indefinite* (**he** vs **someone**), *non-anaphoric* or *anaphoric* (*Why don't* **you** *come?* vs *I'll buy those books because I need* **them**), *independent* or *attributive* (*I want* **that** vs *I want* **that** *book*). Deixis is not referentially restricted to entities; it may also be used for instance, for spatial and temporal qualities. Deictic exponents for each type of notion will be given in the appropriate places.

Division III: Specific notions with recommended exponents for English per topic area

1. Personal identification

1.1	*name*	name
		first name
		surname
		Mr ...
		Mrs ...
		Miss ...
		to write
		How do you write your name?
		names of letters of the alphabet
		to be
		I am Pete Robinson

1.2	*address*	to live
		Where do you live?
		street
		road
		square
		park
		number
		I live at number fifteen
		country
		town
		village
		names of countries
		+ + + + + + + + +

1.3	*telephone number*	telephone
		Have you got a telephone?
		to telephone
		telephone number

1.4	*date and place of birth*	to be born
		I was born in London on 26th July 1930
		names of the months
		the required numerals

| 1.5 | *age* | See II.5.1.10 |

1.6	*sex*	man
		woman
		boy
		girl

| 1.7 | *marital status* | married |
| | | not married |

| 1.8 | *nationality* | names of nationalities |
| | | + + + + + + + + + + |

33

1.9	*origin*	to be + from + NP
		I am from Haarlem
		Where are you from?

1.10	*occupation*	job
		names of occupations
		+ + + + + + + + + +
		to be
		I am a nurse
		office
		shop
		farm
		factory
		school
		hospital
		business
		to work
		I work in a shop
		boss

1.11	*family*	husband
		wife
		father
		mother
		brother
		sister
		child
		son
		daughter

| 1.12 | *religion* | name of one's own religion, if any |
| | | church |

2. House and home

2.1	*accommodation,*	to live
	rooms	*I live in a small house*
		house
		flat
		I live in a flat
		room
		We have two rooms on the ground floor
		kitchen
		bathroom
		bedroom
		living-room
		toilet
		garden
		floor
		The bedrooms are on the first floor
		ground floor

34

		stairs
		lift
		window
		door
2.2	*furniture, bedclothes*	table
		bed
		chair
		light
		Turn on the light, please
		sheet
		blanket
		pillow
2.3	*services*	water
		gas
		electricity
		heating
		telephone
		to turn on
		Turn on the light, please
		to turn off
		How do you turn off the heating?
2.4	*amenities*	bath
		shower
		radio
		television
		garage
2.5	*region*	lake
		hill
		mountain
		fields
		beach
		sea
		near the sea
		island
		river
2.6	*flora and fauna*	flower
		tree
		grass
		animal
		bird
		insect
		fly
		dog
		cat
		horse

3. Free time, entertainment

3.1	*leisure*	holiday(s)
		weekend
		free
		I am free on Saturdays
3.2	*entertainment*	radio
		television
		programme
		There was a nice programme last night
		news
		I always listen to the news
		to watch
		I often watch television
		music
		to sing
		song
		to go out
		We like to go out in the evening
		cinema
		film
		theatre
		ticket
		I had tickets for the cinema
		to dance
		friend
		I go out with friends
3.3	*sports*	sport(s)
		to play
		I don't play football
		against
		England plays against France
		to win
		to lose
		names of sports
		+ + + + + + + +
3.4	*intellectual pursuits*	to read
		to learn
		I'm learning English
		book
3.5	*press*	newspaper
		magazine
		picture

4. Travel

4.1	*public transport*	to go
		How can I go to Liverpool?

to come
I've come to London by air
by (train, car, etc)
by air
plane
train
tram
bus
coach
underground
taxi
boat
station
Where is the station?
airport
bus stop
ticket
return
single
to be
How much is it to Liverpool?
class
I go second class
to buy
to pay
to change
For Leeds you have to change at Sheffield
platform
The train leaves from platform six
to smoke
You may smoke here
journey
tourist

4.2	*private transport*	car
		bicycle
		road
		motorway
		to drive
		to park
		motorbike
		petrol
		oil
4.3	*travel documents*	passport
		insurance
		ticket
4.4	*hotel, camping site, etc*	hotel
		camping site
		tent

room
Have you a room for one night?
single room
double room
to book
I have booked two rooms
front
I'd like a room at the front
back
I'd like a room at the back
bill
Can you give me my bill, please?
key
with or without breakfast
breakfast
lunch
dinner
meal
luggage
suitcase
bag

5. Health and welfare

5.1   *parts of the body*

head
back
I have got a pain in my back
arm
hand
leg
foot
heart
tooth
hair
stomach

5.2   *ailments, accidents*

ill
pain
accident
to break
cold
I have got a cold
to fall
He fell on the ice
to burn
I've burnt my hand
to cut
I've cut my finger
What's the matter?

5.3	*personal comfort*	thirsty
		hungry
		tired
		to sleep
		to wake up
		I woke up at six

5.4	*hygiene*	to wash
		I'd like to wash before dinner
		Can you wash these clothes for me?
		soap
		towel
		toothbrush
		toothpaste
		comb
		razor

5.5	*medical services*	doctor
		dentist
		hospital
		chemist
		medicine
		Take this medicine three times a day
		glasses
		I have broken my glasses

5.6	*emergency services*	police
		policeman
		police station
		fire
		ambulance

6. Shopping

6.1	*shopping facilities*	shop
		supermarket
		market
		We buy our vegetables at the market
		to buy
		to sell
		to pay (+ for + NP)
		Where do I pay
		Where can I pay for this?
		to show
		Can you show me another one?

6.2	*foodstuffs*	see 7.1

6.3	*clothes, fashion*	clothes
		dress
		suit
		underwear

39

trousers
jacket
shirt
blouse
shoe
socks
tights
coat
skirt
size
Size 41, please
to try on
to put on (clothes)
to take off (clothes)
watch
I want to buy a new watch

6.4	*household articles*	spoon
		fork
		knife
		cup
		bottle
		glass
		I want a glass of water
		plate
		Be careful, the plate is hot

6.5	*prices*	See also II.5.2.1
		money
		£
		penny/pence

7. Food and drink

7.1	*types of food and drink*	food
		meal
		to eat
		to drink
		meat
		kinds of meat
		+ + + + + + +
		fish
		chicken
		egg
		vegetables
		kinds of vegetables
		+ + + + + + + + + +
		fruit
		kinds of fruit
		+ + + + + + +
		roast
		I'd like some roast chicken
		grilled

fried
boiled
omelette
sandwich
salt
pepper
mustard
soup
bread
butter
cheese
ice-cream
coffee
tea
milk
sugar
wine
beer
juice
water

7.2	*eating and drinking out*	restaurant
		menu
		May I have the menu, please?
		to have (a meal)
		breakfast
		lunch
		dinner

8. Services

8.1	*post*	post office
		letter
		I want to send a letter to England
		stamp
		I want to buy some stamps
		postcard
8.2	*telephone*	see III.1.3
8.3	*telegraph*	telegram
8.4	*bank*	bank
		Where is the nearest bank?
		money
		to change (money)
		cheque
8.5	*police*	See also III.5.6
		to steal
		to lose
		I've lost my passport

9. Places

See also II.2.1 – II.2.6, III.1.2, III.1.5
map
to cross
We crossed the river at Reading
to pass
We passed a petrol station
bridge
corner
traffic lights
way
Is this the way to the railway station?
<u>Can you tell me the way to . . .?</u>

10. Language

10.1   *ability*

to read
to write
to speak
to understand
language
to know
I don't know that word
word

10.2   *understanding*

to be
What is that in English?
to say again
Please, say that again
<u>Pardon?</u>
to mean
What does this word mean?
to understand
I don't understand this word
slowly
Please, speak very slowly

10.3   *correctness*

right
Is that the right word?
wrong
to pronounce

11. Weather

cold
hot
dry
wet
windy
rain
to rain
weather

fine
The weather is going to be fine tomorrow
sun
snow
to snow
wind
fog
ice
dark
light
It was light at five o'clock

12. Public notices (for reading only)

12.1	*general locations etc*	bus stop
		cloakroom
		closed
		danger
		down
		entrance
		exit
		fire (exit)
		emergency exit
		full
		G (= ground floor)
		ladies
		lift
		lost property office
		men's
		off
		on
		open
		pay here
		police
		post office
		pull
		push
		taxi
		telephone box
		this way
		toilet(s)
		up
		way in
		way out
12.2	*airport*	check in
		departure lounge

1.23	*station*	left-luggage office
		platform
		ticket office
		waiting room
12.4	*hotel*	keys
		lift
		reception
12.5	*on the road*	cross now
		give way
		keep left
		keep right
		no parking
		no waiting
		one way
		stop
		turn left
		turn right
12.6	*prohibitions*	No camping
		No parking
		No smoking
		No swimming
		No waiting

4. LEXICAL INVENTORY

The items are arranged alphabetically. For several items, especially those which may belong to more than one grammatical category or which may have more than one meaning a context is provided in order to indicate the category or the meaning which falls within the objective. See Chapter 5 for a more detailed account of the range of structurally complex items.

a(n)	*Take this medicine three times a day*	II.3.15
a(n)	*I want a glass of beer*	II.4.2.
	I'd like to buy a new suit	II.8
about	*I have about £10*	II.4.1
about	*He talked about his work*	II.7.6.8.
accident		III.5.2
adult	*Adults 50p, children 20p*	II.5.1.9
after	*B comes after A*	II.2.7, II.3.3
afternoon	*Good afternoon!*	I.6.1.
	I went/will go to London this afternoon	II.3.1
	The weather is nice this afternoon	II.3.7
again	*Please, say that again*	II.3.20, III.10.2
against	*England plays against France*	III.3.3
ago	*I was here four days ago*	II.3.1
airport		III.4.1
all	*They all went home*	II.8
	I want all of it	
all	*I've lost all my money*	II.4.2
almost		II.4.3
already	*I have already done it*	II.3.2
always		II.3.15, II.3.18, II.8
am	*It's three am*	II.3.1
	At three am	
ambulance		III.5.6
and		II.7.6.1
animal		III.2.6
another	*May I have another cup of tea?*	II.4.1
	Give me another (= different) book	II.7.4.1
any	*There isn't any milk*	II.1.1, II.1.3
	Have you got any sugar	II.4.2
anything		II.8
April		II.3.1
arm		III.5.1
arrive	*The train arrived at eleven*	II.2.4
ask	*May I ask a question?*	II.6.2
at	*We are going to wait at the station*	II.2.2
	He is at home	
at	*I saw him at four o'clock*	II.3.1
August		II.3.1
autumn		II.3.1

away	*He's not here. He's away*	II.1.2
	He walked away	II.2.5
away	*It's two miles away*	II.2.3
back	*We went back*	II.2.5
back	*I'd like a room at the back*	III.4.4
back	*I have got a pain in my back*	III.5.1
bad		II.5.2.2
badly		II.7.3.8
bag		III.4.4
bank	*Where is the nearest bank?*	III.8.4
bath		III.2.4
bathroom		III.2.1
be	*This/that is (very) nice*	I.3.1
	How are you?	I.6.2
	I'm fine, thank you, how are you?	
be	*There is some sugar in the kitchen*	III.1.1
be	*How much is it to Liverpool?*	III.4.1
	How much are these shoes?	II.5.2.1
be	*I am from Haarlem*	III.1.9
	Where are you from?	
be	*I am a nurse*	III.1.10
be	*I am Pete Robinson*	III.1.1
	What is that in English?	III.10.2
be born	*I was born in London on 26 July 1930*	III.1.4
be going to	*The train is going to be late*	II.3.6
beach		III.2.5
because		II.7.6.4, II.7.6.6
bed		III.2.2
bedroom		III.2.1
beer		III.7.1.
before	*A comes before B*	II.2.7, II.3.2
behind	*There's a tree behind the house*	II.2.2
best		II.5.2.2
better	*Your English is better now*	II.5.2.2, II.5.2.5
between	*Henley is between London and Oxford*	II.2.2
	B comes between A and C	II.2.7
bicycle		III.4.2
big		II.2.8.1, II.2.8.6
bill	*Can you give me my bill, please?*	III.4.4
bird		III.2.6
black		II.5.1.8
blanket		III.2.2
blouse		III.6.3
blue		II.5.1.8
boat		III.4.1
boiled	*I'd like a boiled egg, please*	III.7.1
book	*I want to buy an English book*	III.3.4
book	*I have booked two rooms*	III.4.4
boss		III.1.10

bottle		III.6.4
boy		III.1.6
bread		III.7.1
break	*He has broken his leg*	II.5.1.10, III.5.2
breakfast		III.4.4, III.7.2
bridge	*There's a bridge at Marlow*	III.9
bring	*Bring me some water*	II.2.5
brother		III.1.11
brown		II.5.1.8
burn	*I've burnt my hand*	III.5.2
bus		III.4.1
bus stop		III.4.1
business		III.1.10
but	*I want a new car, but I have not got any money*	II.7.6.1
butter		III.7.1
buy		III.4.1, III.6.1
by	*I've come to London by air*	III.4.1
camping site		III.4.4
can	*Can you speak French?*	I.2.7, I.2.8, II.5.2.6
can	*Can I help you?*	I.5.4
can	*Can you help me?*	I.5.5
can	*Can I play football tomorrow?*	I.2.12
car		III.4.2
careful	*Be careful!*	I.5.2
cat		III.2.6
centimetre		II.2.8.2
centre	*I live in the centre of Manchester*	II.2.2
chair		III.2.2
change	*The weather has changed*	II.3.24
change	*I want to change 50 German Marks*	III.8.4
change	*For Leeds you have to change at Sheffield*	III.4.1
cheap		II.5.2.1
cheers		I.6.6
cheese		III.7.1
chemist		III.5.5
cheque		III.8.4
chicken		III.7.1
child		II.5.1.9, III.1.11
church		III.1.12
cinema		III.3.2
class	*I go second class*	III.4.1
clean	*This shirt is not clean*	II.5.1.12
clean	*She cleans the house every week*	II.5.1.12
closed	*This door is closed*	II.5.1.11
clothes		III.6.3
coat		III.6.3
coffee		III.7.1
cold	*It's very cold today*	II.2.8.7, III.11

cold	I have got a cold	III.5.2
colour	That is a nice colour	II.5.1.8
comb	I've lost by comb	III.5.4
come	He came very late	II.2.4
	He came to our house	
	I've come to London by air	
corner	The restaurant is at the corner	III.9
cotton		II.5.1.13
country	Luxembourg is a small country	III.1.2
cross	We crossed the river at Reading	III.9
cup		III.6.4
cut	I have cut my hand	II.5.1.10, III.5.2
dance	Do you like to dance	III.3.2
dark	It is too dark in here	II.5.1.4, III.11
dark	I want a dark colour	II.5.1.8
daughter		III.1.11
day		II.3.13
dead	The dog is dead	II.5.1.10
December		II.3.1
dentist		III.5.5
different		II.7.4.1, II.7.4.2
difficult		II.5.2.9
dinner		III.4.4, III.7.2
do	Do you know him?	I.1.4, I.2.4
	I don't know him	I.1.3, I.2.2, I.2.3
	It doesn't matter	I.4.6
do	How do you do?	I.6.3
do	What are you going to do tonight?	II.8
doctor		III.5.5
dog		III.2.6
door		III.2.1
double	I've booked a double room	III.4.4
down	I am going down	II.2.5
dress	She bought a new dress	III.6.3
drink	You cannot drink this water	III.7.1
drive	Can't you drive faster?	III.4.2
dry	It will be dry tomorrow	II.5.1.3, III.11
dry	Where can I dry my clothes?	II.5.1.3
early	You are early	II.3.11
	There is an early train on Mondays	
	You came too early	
east	He lives in the east (of England)	II.2.1
easy		II.5.2.9
eat		III.7.1
egg		III.7.1
electricity		III.2.3
empty	The bottle is empty	II.5.1.14
end	The hotel is at the end of the street	II.2.2
enough	I haven't got enough money	II.4.2

48

	It's enough	II.5.2.4
evening	*Good evening*	I.6.1
	What are you going to do this evening?	II.3.1
every		II.3.15
excuse	*Excuse me, please*	I.6.5
expensive		II.5.2.1
factory		III.1.10
fall	*He fell on the ice*	III.5.2
far	*We don't live far from the station*	II.2.3
farm		III.1.10
fast	*This is a very fast car*	II.3.14
father		III.1.11
February		II.3.1
few		II.4.2
a few		II.4.2
fields		III.2.5
fill		II.5.1.14
film	*I saw a nice film last night*	III.3.2
fine	*The weather is going to be fine tomorrow*	III.11
fine	*I'm fine, thank you*	I.6.2
fire		III.5.6
first	*John came first*	II.2.7
	First we went to London	II.3.4
first name		III.1.1
fish	*I'd like some fried fish*	III.7.1
flat	*I live in a flat*	III.2.1
floor	*The bedrooms are on the first floor*	III.2.1
flower		III.2.6
fly	*There's a fly in your soup*	III.2.6
fog		III.11
food		III.7.1
foot	*I've cut my foot*	III.5.1
foot	*The car is thirteen ft long*	II.2.8.2
for	*I've been here for two hours*	II.3.16, II.3.19
for	*I have bought this for my wife*	II.7.3.5
fork		III.6.4
free	*I am free on Saturdays*	III.3.1
Friday		II.3.1
fried	*I'd like some fried fish*	III.7.1
friend	*I go out with friends*	III.3.2
from	*He has come from London*	II.2.5
	I come from London	II.2.6
front	*I'd like a room at the front*	III.4.4
in front of	*There's a tree in front of the house*	II.2.2
fruit		III.7.1
full		II.5.1.14
gallon		II.2.8.5
garage		III.2.4
garden		III.2.1, III.2.3

49

get	*I got a nice present from him*	II.7.5.1
get up	*I have to get up at six*	II.2.4
girl		III.1.6
give	*I gave him a nice present*	II.7.5.1
glass	*I want a glass of water*	III.6.4
glasses	*I have broken my glasses*	III.5.5
go	*Where did you go last night?*	II.2.4
	He went into the house	
	How can I go to Liverpool?	III.4.1
go home		II.2.4
go out	*We like to go out in the evening*	II.2.4, III.3.2
go away		II.2.4
going to	*I'm going to help you*	I.3.9
	It's going to rain	II.3.6
good	*That's very good*	I.3.4, II.5.2.2
	Good!	I.4.3
good-bye		I.6.4
gram(me)		II.2.8.4
grass		III.2.6
green		II.5.1.8
grey		II.5.1.8
grilled		III.7.1
ground floor		III.2.1
hair		III.5.1
half	*It's half past three*	II.3.1
half	*Give me half of it*	II.4.2
	Give me the other half	
	Give me half a bottle	
hallo		I.6.1, I.6.2
hand	*I've burnt my hand*	III.5.1
happen	*What happened*	I.1.2
hard	*This pillow is too hard*	II.5.1.7
have	*I have (got) a small car*	II.1.3, II.7.5.1
have	*I have been to Paris*	II.2.1, II.3.2
	I haven't seen John yet	
have (a meal)	*Let's have breakfast at eight*	III.7.2
have to		I.2.10
he		I.1.1, II.8
head		III.5.1
hear		II.5.1.5
heart		III.5.1
heating	*There's no heating in this room*	III.2.3
heavy	*This blanket is too heavy*	II.2.8.4
help	*Can I help you?*	I.5.4
her	*Give me her book*	II.7.5.1, II.8
here		II.1.2, II.2.1, II.8
hers		II.7.5.1, II.8
high		II.2.8.1
hill		III.2.5

50

him		II.8
his	*Give me his book*	II.7.5.1, II.8
	It's his	
holiday(s)		III.3.1
home	*He's at home*	II.2.2
	I go home at six	II.2.4
hope	*I hope that you can help me*	II.6.1
horse		III.2.6
hospital		III.1.10, III.5.5
hot		II.2.8.7, III.11
hotel		III.4.4
hour		II.3.13
house		III.2.1
how	*How far is it?*	I.1.4
	How much are these shoes?	II.5.2.1
	How can I do it?	II.7.3.8
How are you?		I.6.2
How do you do?		I.6.3
hungry		III.5.3
husband		III.1.11
I		I.1.1, II.8
ice		III.11
ice-cream		III.7.1
ill	*Are you ill?*	II.5.1.10, III.5.2
important		II.5.2.7
in	*I'll see you in July*	II.3.1
	I'll see you in four days	II.3.6
in	*I live in London*	II.2.2
in	*Don't go in now*	II.2.5
inch		II.2.8.2
insect		III.2.6
inside	*Come inside*	II.2.1
inside	*My car is inside*	II.2.2
insurance		III.4.3
into	*He went into the house*	II.2.5
island		III.2.5
it	*It is a very nice picture*	I.1.1, II.8
it	*It's raining*	II.8
jacket		III.6.3
January		II.3.1
job		III.1.10
journey		III.4.1
juice		III.7.1
July		II.3.1
June		II.3.1
just	*I've just seen him*	II.3.8
keep	*May I keep this?*	II.7.5.1
key		III.4.4
kilo(gram)		II.2.8.4

kilometre		II.2.8.2
kitchen		III.2.1
knife		III.6.4
know	*I don't know that word*	I.2.3, II.6.1, II.10.1
lake		III.2.5
language		III.10.1
last	*I saw him last week (month, year)*	II.3.1, II.3.8
last	*Peter came last*	II.2.7
late	*The train is going to be late*	II.3.10
	We were too late for the train	II.3.12
later	*I'm going to do this later*	II.3.3
learn	*I'm learning English*	III.3.4
leave	*We left the station at ten*	II.2.4
left	*Turn left at the crossing*	II.2.5
leg		III.5.1
let's	*Let's have breakfast at eight*	I.5.6
letter	*I want to send a letter to England*	III.8.1
lift	*Take the lift to the sixth floor*	III.2.1
light	*It's light at five am in summer*	II.5.1.4, III.11
light	*I want a light colour*	II.5.1.8
light	*I want a very light blanket*	II.2.8.4
light	*Turn on the light, please*	III.2.2
like	*I like you*	I.3.1
	Would you like to go out tonight?	I.3.12
listen	*Listen to me, please*	II.5.1.5
	Listen, it is raining	
litre		II.2.8.5
little	*I have little money*	II.4.2
a little	*I have a little money*	II.4.2
	I'm a little better	II.4.3
live	*Where do you live?*	III.1.2
	I live in a small house	III.2.1
living room		III.2.1
long	*This road is very long*	II.2.8.2
long	*We had to wait a long time*	II.3.13
look	*Don't look now!*	II.5.1.4
	Look at his new car	
look out!		I.5.2
lose	*England has lost the game*	III.3.3
lose	*I've lost my passport*	III.8.5
a lot of		II.4.2
loud	*The music is too loud*	II.5.1.5
low		II.2.8.1
luggage		III.4.4
lunch		III.4.4, III.7.2
magazine	*I'd like to buy some magazines*	III.3.5
make	*She made a new dress*	II.1.1
man		III.1.6
many	*I've seen him many times*	II.3.20

52

	He hasn't got many friends	II.4.2
map	I've bought a new map of England	III.9
March		II.3.1
market	We buy our vegetables at the market	III.6.1
married	Are you married?	III.1.7
matter	What's the matter?	III.5.2
matter	It doesn't matter	I.4.6
may (permission)	May I put my coat here?	I.2.12
may (request)	May I have another cup of tea?	I.3.11
May		II.3.1
me		II.8
meal	Can I have a meal here?	III.4.4, III.7.1
mean	What does this word mean?	III.10.2
meat		III.7.1
medicine	Take this medicine three times a day	III.5.5
menu	May I have the menu, please?	III.7.2
metre		II.2.8.2
mile		II.2.8.2
milk	A glass of milk, please	III.7.1
mine	This is mine	II.7.5.1, II.8
minute		II.3.13
Miss		III.1.1
Monday		II.3.1
money		III.6.5, III.8.4
month		II.3.1, II.3.13
more	I want more stamps	II.4.2
morning	Good morning!	I.6.1
	I saw them this morning	II.3.1
most	Most shops are closed on Sundays	II.4.2
mother		III.1.11
motor-bike		III.4.2
motorway		III.4.2
mountain		III.2.5
Mr		III.1.1
Mrs		III.1.1
much	There isn't much bread	II.4.2
	This is much better	II4.3
	How much are these shoes?	II.5.2.1
music		III.3.2
mustard		III.7.1
my		II.7.5.1, II.8
name		III.1.1
near	We live near the railway station	II.2.3
never	I never play football	I.1.3, I.2.2, II.3.15
		II.8
new	We have got a new car	II.5.1.9
news	I always listen to the news	III.3.2
newspaper		III.3.5

next	*I'll see you next week*	II.3.1, II.3.6
next to	*The garage is next to the hotel*	II.2.2
nice	*That's very nice*	I.3.1, I.3.4, I.4.4,
	This meat is (not) very nice	II.5.1.6
night	*I saw him last night*	II.3.1
no	*No, thank you*	I.1.4, I.2.6
no	*There is no beer*	I.1.3, II.4.2
noise	*There is too much noise here*	II.5.1.5
north	*He lives in the north (of England)*	II.2.1
not	*There is not any beer*	I.1.3, II.4.2
	John has not seen him	
nothing		I.1.3, II.8
November		II.3.1
now		II.3.1, II.3.7, II.8
number	*I live at number fifteen*	III.1.2
nylon		II.5.1.13
o'clock	*It's four o'clock*	II.3.1
October		II.3.1
of		II.7.5.1
office		III.1.10
often		II.3.15
old	*I am too old for this*	II.5.1.9
	How old are you?	
	This house is 150 years old	
omelette		III.7.1
on	*The food was on the table*	II.2.2
on	*I'll see you on Monday*	II.3.1
once	*I've been here only once*	II.3.21
one	*I'll be in London for one day*	II.4.1
	May I have the red one, please?	II.8
only	*Milk? Only a little please*	II.7.6.8
open	*The door is open*	II.5.1.11
or		II.7.6.2
orange	*Orange is a nice colour*	II.5.1.8
other	*Give me the other book*	II.7.4.1
ounce (oz)		II.2.8.4
our		II.7.5.1, II.8
ours		II.7.5.1, II.8
out	*We walked out*	II.2.5
	We like to go out in the evening	II.2.4, III.3.2
out of	*He came out of the house*	II.2.5
outside	*Let's go outside*	II.2.1
outside	*My wife is outside*	II.2.2
pain		III.5.2
pair	*I want to buy a pair of shoes*	II.7.6.1
paper	*It's only a paper bag*	II.5.1.13
pardon	*Pardon?*	III.10.2
park	*My house is near Hyde Park*	III.1.2
park	*Where can I park my car?*	III.4.2

54

pass	*We passed a petrol station*	III.9
passport		III.4.3
past	*It's a quarter past three*	II.3.1
pay	*Where do I pay?*	III.4.1, III.6.1
	Where can I pay for this?	
pence		III.6.5
penny		III.6.5
people	*There are five people here*	II.8
pepper		III.7.1
perhaps		I.2.9
petrol		III.4.2
picture	*Have you seen her picture in the newspaper?*	III.3.5
piece	*I would like a piece of cheese*	II.4.2
pillow		III.2.2
pint		II.2.8.5
pity	*What a pity!*	I.3.6, I.4.5
plane	*Our plane leaves at five*	III.4.1
plastic		II.5.1.13
plate	*Be careful, the plate is hot*	III.6.4
platform	*The train leaves from platform six*	III.4.1
play	*I don't play football*	III.3.3
please	*Yes please*	I.2.5
	I'd like some milk, please	I.3.11
	Please help me	I.5.1
pm	*It's three pm now*	II.3.1
	At three pm	
police		III.5.6
policeman		III.5.6
police station		III.5.6
postcard		III.8.1
post office		III.8.1
pound (£)		III.6.5
pound (lb)		II.2.8.4
prefer	*I('d) prefer a cup of tea*	I.3.7
programme	*There was a nice programme last night*	III.3.2
pronounce		III.10.3
put	*May I put my coat here?*	II.2.5
put on	*Put on your coat*	III.6.3
quarter	*It's a quarter to three*	II.3.1
question	*May I ask a question?*	II.6.2
quickly		II.7.3.8
radio		III.2.4, III.3.2
rain	*We had too much rain last week*	III.11
rain	*It is raining again*	III.11
razor		III.5.4
read		III.3.4, III.10.1
ready	*When will it be ready?*	II.1.3
red		II.5.1.8
restaurant		III.7.2

return	*I'd like a return ticket to London*	III.4.1
right	*All right*	I.2.1, I.2.12
	That's all right	I.4.2, II.5.2.3
	It's all right	II.5.2.4
	He/His car is all right now	II.5.1.10
	Is that the right word?	II.5.2.5, III.10.3
right	*Turn right at the crossing*	II.2.5
river		III.2.5
road		III.1.2, III.4.2
roast	*I'd like some roast chicken*	III.7.1
room	*We have two rooms on the ground floor*	III.2.1
	Have you a room for one night?	III.4.4
double room		III.4.4
single room		III.4.4
round	*It's round*	II.5.1.1
salt		III.7.1
same	*This book is the same as that*	II.7.4.1
	They are not the same	II.7.4.2
	They came at the same time	II.3.5
sandwich		III.7.1
Saturday		II.3.1
say	*How do you say that in English?*	II.6.2
school		III.1.10
sea	*We live near the sea*	III.2.5
see	*I can see you*	II.5.1.4
sell		III.6.1
send	*I want to send a letter to Holland*	II.2.5
September		II.3.1
service	*Is this the price with or without service?*	III.4.4
she		I.1.1, II.8
sheet	*I'll put a clean sheet on your bed*	III.2.2
shirt		III.6.3
shoe		III.6.3
shop	*I bought the shoes in that shop*	III.1.10, III.6.1
short	*I want a short coat*	II.2.8.2
short	*We waited a short time*	II.3.13
show	*Can you show me another one?*	III.6.1
shower	*I'd like a room with a shower*	III.2.4
since	*I've been here since yesterday*	II.3.13, II.3.22
sing		III.3.2
single	*Please give me a single to London*	III.4.1
	I've booked a single room	III.4.4
sister		III.1.11
sit	*Don't sit on that table!*	II.2.4
sit down	*I'd like to sit down now*	II.2.4
size	*Size 41, please*	III.6.3
skirt		III.6.3
sleep	*I could not sleep last night*	III.5.3
slow	*This is a slow train*	II.3.14

56

slowly	*Please, speak very slowly*	II.7.3.8, III.10.2
small		II.2.8.1, II.2.8.6
smoke	*You may smoke here*	III.4.1
snow	*There is snow on the mountains*	III.11
snow	*It will snow tomorrow*	III.11
so	*He didn't arrive so I left*	II.7.6.5
so	*He wanted to leave, but he didn't say so*	II.8
soap		III.5.4
socks		III.6.3
soft	*I want a soft pillow*	II.5.1.7
some	*Bring me some water*	II.4.2
	I want to buy some stamps	
something		II.8
sometimes		II.3.15, II.8
son		III.1.11
song		III.3.2
soon		II.3.6
sorry	*I'm (very) sorry*	I.4.1
soup		III.7.1
south	*He lives in the south (of England)*	II.2.1
speak	*Can you speak French?*	II.6.2, III.10.1
spoon		III.6.4
sport(s)		III.3.3
spring	*We have nice flowers in spring*	II.3.1
square	*I live in Portman Square*	III.1.2
square	*This piece of cheese is square*	II.5.1.1
stairs		III.2.1
stamp	*I want to buy some stamps*	III.8.1
stand	*I had to stand in the train*	II.2.4
start	*The journey started at seven*	II.3.22
	He started to speak	
station	*Where is the station?*	III.4.1
stay	*I'm going to stay here for a week*	II.2.4
	It is not going to stay dry today	
steal		III.8.5
still	*He is still working*	II.3.7
stomach		III.5.1
stop	*The car stopped in front of a garage*	II.2.4, II.3.23
straight on		II.2.5
strange		II.5.2.8
street		III.1.2
strong	*This is very strong plastic*	II.5.1.7
suddenly		II.3.24
sugar		III.7.1
suit	*This suit is too small*	III.6.3
suitcase		III.4.4
summer		II.3.1
sun		III.11
Sunday		II.3.1

57

supermarket		III.6.1
surname		III.1.1
table	*I'll put the flowers on the table*	III.2.2
take	*How long does it take?*	II.3.13
	It takes five minutes (by taxi)	
take	*I'd like to take this with me*	II.2.5
take off	*Take off your coat*	III.6.3
talk	*We talked for a long time*	II.6.2
taxi		III.4.1
tea		III.7.1
telegram		III.8.3
telephone	*Have you got a telephone?*	III.1.3, III.2.3, III.8
telephone	*I'd like to telephone to Italy*	III.1.3, III.8.2
telephone number		III.1.3
television		III.2.4, III.3.2
tell	*Tell me about your work*	II.6.2
tent		III.4.4
than	*John is older than his brother*	II.7.4.2
thank	*Thank you*	I.2.5, I.2.6, I.3.8
	No, thank you	
	I'd like to thank you	
that	*I want that book*	I.1.1, II.2.1, II.8
that	*I think that she is at home now*	I.2.9
the		II.8
theatre		II.3.2
their		II.7.5.1, II.8
theirs		II.7.5.1, II.8
them		II.8
then	*Then we went home*	II.3.1, II.8
	First we went to London, then we went to	II.3.4
	Paris	II.7.6.5
	He ate too much ice-cream and then he was ill	
there	*There is no water in this room*	II.1.1, II.1.3
there	*There he is!*	II.2.1, II.8
	The book is there	
these		I.1.1, II.2.1, II.8
they		I.1.1, II.8
thing	*What do you call that thing?*	II.8
think	*I think so*	I.2.9, II.6.1
	I think that you are ill	
thirsty		III.5.3
this	*This book is mine*	I.1.1, II.2.1, II.8
	This morning I got up late	II.3.1, II.3.7
those		I.1.1, II.2.1, II.8
through	*He went through the centre of the town*	II.2.5
Thursday		II.3.1
ticket	*I had tickets for the cinema*	III.3.2, III.4.1
	I bought a ticket to London	III.4.3

58

tights		III.6.3
till	*I'll wait till ten o'clock*	II.3.13, II.3.23
time	*What time is it?*	II.3.1
time	*I go to evening classes four times a week*	II.3.15, II.3.20
tired	*Are you tired?*	III.5.3
to	*It's a quarter to three*	II.3.1
to	*This train goes to London*	II.2.5
to	*He gave the ticket to my brother*	II.7.3.3
to	*He came to help me*	II.7.6.7
today		II.3.1, II.3.7
toilet		III.2.1
tomorrow		II.3.1, II.3.6
tonight		II.3.1, II.3.6
too	*This blanket is too heavy*	II.4.3
too	*John is going to come too*	II.7.6.1
tooth		III.5.1
toothbrush		III.5.4
toothpaste		III.5.4
tourist		III.4.1
towel		III.5.4
town		III.1.2
traffic lights		III.9
train	*We went to Sheffield by train*	III.4.1
tram		III.4.1
tree		III.2.5
trousers		III.6.3
try on		III.6.3
Tuesday		II.3.1
turn	*Turn right at the river*	II.2.5
turn on	*Turn on the light, please*	III.2.3
Turn off	*How do you turn off the heating?*	III.2.3
twice		II.3.20
under	*The dog was under the table*	II.2.2
underground	*Take the underground to Oxford Circus*	III.4.1
understand	*I don't understand this word*	III.10.1, III.10.2
underwear		III.6.3
up	*Are you going up?*	II.2.5
us		II.8
usually		II.3.15
vegetables		III.7.1
very		II.4.3
village		III.1.2
wait	*We had to wait five minutes*	II.2.4
	Wait for me, please	
wake up	*I woke up at six*	III.5.3
walk	*We are going to walk to the railway station*	II.2.4
want	*I want a short coat*	I.3.11
	I want to leave	
warm	*Put a warm coat on*	II.2.8.7

59

wash	I'd like to wash before dinner	II.5.1.12, III.5.4
	Can you wash these clothes for me?	
watch	I often watch television	III.3.2
watch	I want to buy a new watch	III.6.3
water	Can I have some water, please?	III.2.3, III.7.1
way	Is this the way to the railway station?	III.9
	Can you tell me the way to Regent's Park	
we		I.1.1, II.8
weather		III.11
Wednesday		II.3.1
week		II.3.1, II.3.13
weekend		III.3.1
well	I am very well	II.5.1.10
well	He cannot write English very well	II.5.2.2, II.7.3.8
west	He lives in the west (of England)	II.2.1
wet		II.5.1.3, III.11
what	What can I do for you?	I.1.4, II.8
when	When did you arrive?	I.1.4, II.3.1
where	Where is your wife?	I.1.4, II.2.1
which	Which room would you like?	II.8
white		II.5.1.8
who	Who is he?	I.1.4, II.8
whose		II.8
why		I.1.4, II.7.6.4,
		II.7.6.6
wife		III.1.11
win		III.3.3
wind	There's no wind today	III.11
window		III.2.1
wine		III.7.1
winter		II.3.1
with	You can open the door with this key	II.7.3.4
with	We are going to take John with us	II.7.6.3
with	Did you see a man with a big suitcase?	II.7.5.1
without	We cannot go without you	II.7.6.3
without	Don't go there without your passport	II.7.5.1
woman		III.1.6
wool		II.5.1.13
word		III.10.1
work	I work in a shop	III.1.10
would	Would you like ice-cream?	I.3.13
	Would you like to go out tonight?	
write	I want to write a letter	II.6.2
	How do you write your name?	III.1.1
	I cannot write English very well	III.10.1
wrong	The answer is wrong	II.5.2.5, III.10.3
year	We'll go to Italy next year	II.3.1, II.3.13
	This house is (150) years old	II.5.1.9
yellow		II.5.1.8

60

yes		I.2.1, I.2.12
yesterday		II.3.1, II.3.8
yet	*Has he come yet?*	II.3.2
	He has not come yet	
you		I.1.1, II.8
young	*He is very young*	II.5.1.9
your		II.7.5.1, II.8
yours		II.7.5.1, II.8

Public notices (III.12)
(for reading only, unless occurring in other sections as well)

bus stop	III.12.1
check in	III.12.2
cloackroom	III.12.1
closed	III.12.1
cross now	III.12.5
danger	III.12.1
departure lounge	III.12.2
down	III.12.1
entrance	III.12.1
exit	III.12.1
fire (exit)	III.12.1
full	III.12.1
G (= ground floor)	III.12.1
give way	III.12.5
keep left	III.12.5
keep right	III.12.5
keys	III.12.4
ladies	III.12.1
left luggage office	III.12.3
lift	III.12.1
lost property office	III.12.1
men's	III.12.1
No camping	III.12.6
No parking	III.12.5, III.12.6
No smoking	III.12.6
No swimming	III.12.6
off	III.12.1
on	III.12.1
one way	III.12.5
open	III.12.1
pay here	III.12.1
platform	III.12.3
police	III.12.1

post office	III.12.1
pull	III.12.1
push	III.12.1
reception	III.12.4
stop	III.12.5
taxi	III.12.1
telephone box	III.12.1
this way	III.12.1
ticket office	III.12.3
toilet(s)	III.12.1
turn left	III.12.5
turn right	III.12.5
up	III.12.1
waiting	III.12.3
way in	III.12.1
way out	III.12.1

Weights and measures

length (II.2.8.2) *weight* (II.2.8.4)   *volume* (II.2.8.5)

length	weight	volume
centimetre	gram(me)	gallon
foot	kilo	litre
inch	ounce (oz)	pint
kilometre	pound (lb)	
metre		
mile		

Open-ended items

Names of countries	III.1.2
Names of nationalities	III.1.8
Names of occupations	III.1.10
Names of sports	III.3.3
Kinds of meat	III.7.1
Kinds of vegetables	III.7.1
Kinds of fruit	III.7.1

5. STRUCTURAL INVENTORY

This is an inventory and not a reference grammar: that is, it does not set out to provide information about the use of English. It is assumed that the potential user is reasonably conversant with English grammatical structure. The listed items and their exponents are not meant to be in any way exhaustive or prescriptive. They merely demonstrate the range of structures and possible utterances that would have to be taught if Waystage specifications were assumed.

An alphabetical ordering has been preferred to any other form of presentation since it is the least prescriptive model. It can be manipulated creatively by the user who is free to decide on his own sequence for teaching purposes. A two-column layout has been adopted: the items to be considered are on the left and their possible exponents are on the right. All structural words and problematical lexical items are given in BLOCK CAPITALS and all grammatical categories in light-face Roman; exponents are *in italics*.

When using this inventory, the following should be noted:

1. A great many (though by no means all) of the structural words and problematical lexical items which appear in the lexicon are listed in this inventory. Occasionally, single items (eg 'give') are included to represent a particular grammatical category and the use is referred to the relevant entries.

2. Compounds and derivatives are possible providing that their meaning is fully predictable from the content specification. For instance, 'put up (your hand)' would fall within Waystage specifications even though it is not listed in the *Lexicon* or in this inventory, but 'put up with' (=*tolerate*) would not.

A, AN
    indefinite article: *I am a policeman*
    distributive: *Take this medicine three times a day*
    after HALF/WHAT: *Give me half a bottle*
                                    What a pity!

Ability   See CAN

ABOUT
    (=APPROXIMATELY):   *I have about $25*
    (=CONCERNING):   *He talked about his work*

Addresses   *I live at number 15 Church Road*

Adjectives   *I want a short coat*
    attributive/predicative: *This is nice*
    comparison: See under: Comparative forms
    possessive: See: Pronouns

Adverbial
    form: + -ly: *badly, slowly, quickly*
    particle: *Sit down/Wake up*
    of degree: *It's very hot*

Adverbial (*contd.*)
    of frequency: *He's always late*
    of manner: *well, badly, slowly, quickly*
                                         I've come to London by air
    of place: *It's here/there in the garden*
    of time: *He arrived today/yesterday*
                                                on Sunday
                                                at four o'clock
                                                in winter
                                                two hours ago

TOO: *John is going to come too*
    transposable particle: *Put on your coat*
                                                  Put your coat on
                                                  Put it on

AGAINST:
    as preposition (opposition):   *England plays against France*

Age   *How old are you?*
                                                This house is 150 years old

AGO
    exact time reference with:
    past tense: *I was in Paris four days ago*

ALL   *They all went home*
                                                I want all of it
                                                All the shops are closed
                                                I've lost all my money

ALMOST   *It's almost full*
                                                I'm almost ready

ALREADY   *I have already done it*

ALWAYS   *He's always late*

AND
    joining words and phrases: *It's black and white*
    joining clauses: *He speaks and writes English*
                                                I'm staying here and John is too

ANOTHER
    (=ONE MORE):   *May I have another cup of tea, please?*
    (=A DIFFERENT):   *Give me another book*

ANY   See: SOME

ANYTHING   See under: SOME compounds

Apostrophe 's'   See: Genitive

Articles   See: A; THE; Zero

ASK   *May I ask a question?*

AT	
referring to place:	*We are going to wait at the station*
	He is at home
referring to time:	*We left the station at ten*
Attributive	See under: Adjective
Auxiliaries	See: BE, DO, HAVE
AWAY	
as particle:	*He walked away*
BACK	
as particle:	*We went back*
BE	
as a full verb:	*That is very nice*
	He's been to Paris
auxiliary:	See: Present perfect; Present progressive
contrasted with GO:	*He's gone to Paris/He's been to Paris*
	Where did you go (last night)?
	Where have you been?
+GOING TO:	See: Future
Imperative:	*Be careful?*
BECAUSE	
as subordinating conj:	*He didn't come because he was ill*
WHY? BECAUSE:	*Why did you leave? Because I was late*
BEEN	See: Present perfect tense
BEHIND	
as preposition:	*There's a tree behind the house*
BETWEEN	*Henley is between London and Oxford*
BRING	*Bring me some water*
	Bring it to me
BUT	*I want a new car, but I have not got any money*
BY	
in adv phrases of manner:	*I've come to London by air*
CAN	
ability:	*Can you speak French?*
in offers of help:	*Can I help you?*
giving and seeking permission:	*You can have my car for a week*
Cardinal numbers	Up to four digits
CLAUSES	
cause/reason: BECAUSE:	*He hasn't come because he's ill*
	Why isn't he here? Because he's ill
purpose: TO:	*He came to help me*
result: SO:	*He ate too much so he didn't feel well*
THAT:	*I hope that you can help me*

COME
    from a source/origin: *I come from London*
    + HOME: *He came home late*
                                     See: GO
    + TO + NP: *He came to our house*

Comparative forms
    Adj with: –er (than):   *John is older than his brother*
            –est: *Where is the nearest bank?*
            –y/–ier: *I want a heavier coat*
      irregular forms: better/best

Compounds of SOME, ANY, NO   See under SOME compounds

Compound nouns   eg POST OFFICE, BUS STOP

Concord, eg   *Jane is a nurse. Mary is a nurse*
                                     Jane and Mary are nurses
                                     I want a cup of coffee
                                     He wants a cup of coffee
                                     I don't smoke
                                     He doesn't smoke

Conjunctions   See; AND; BUT; OR; SO

Continuous tenses   See; Present progressive

Contractions, eg   *I'm going to do this later*
                                     It doesn't matter
                                     I've lived here for two years
                                     I'd like a room at the front

Cost/price   *How much are these shoes?*
                                     How much is it to Liverpool?

Countries, eg   *He is from France*

Dates
    spoken convention, eg: *June the thirteenth*
                                     The thirteenth of June
    written convention, eg: *June 13th; June 13; 13th June; 13 June*

Days of the week   (included)

Demonstratives
    adjectives: *This/that car is new*
                                     This/that one is new
                                     These/those cars are new
                                     These/those are new
    pronouns: *Give me this/that one*
                                     What are these/those?

DIFFERENT: *This is different*
                                     This is different from that
                                     See: SAME

Direct object	*He gave the ticket to my brother* Other verbs: SEND *I have bought this for my wife*
Distance	*How far is it?* *It's two miles away*
DO/DID	
as auxiliary: interrogative present and past (yes/no questions):	*Do you know Robert?* *Did you see a man with a big suitcase?*
as auxiliary: negative present and past:	*It doesn't matter* *We don't live far from the station* *He wanted to leave, but he did not say so*
as full verb:	*What are you going to do tonight?* *How can I do it?*
in imperatives (negative):	*Don't sit on that table!*
DOWN	
as adverb particle:	*I'd like to sit down now*
Duration	See under: FOR, SINCE, LONG
ENOUGH	
predicatively:	*It's enough*
as determiner/quantifier:	*I haven't got enough money*
EVERY	*We see him every week*
FAR	
+FROM:	*We don't live far from the station*
FAST	
as adj:	*This is a very fast car*
FEW	
with plural unit nouns:	*There are very few good restaurants here*
A FEW (+A NUMBER OF):	*I know a few good restaurants here* See: LITTLE; Quantifiers
FIRST	
as adj:	*The first book was difficult*
as adv:	*John came first*
as ordinal:	*I saw him on January 1st*
FOR	*I have bought this for my wife*
destination/purpose:	*You can have my car for a week*
duration:	See: Present perfect tense
FROM	
a source/origin:	*I come from London* *Where are you from?*
direction (movement):	*He has come from London*
Future, ways of expressing	
be going to:	*We are going to walk to the station*
will:	*When will it be ready?*

Genitive:
  of personal pronouns: *My name's Tom*
  with apostrophe ('s or s'):   *It's John's book*
                                   It's James'(s) book
                                   I bought it at the chemist's

GET
  referring to possession: *I have got a small car*
  referring to physical action: *I have to get up at six*
  + RECEIVE: *I got a nice present from him*
  + particle: *I have to get up at six*

GIVE   See: Direct object, Indirect object

GO
  (= DEPART):   *Where did you go (last night)?*
                               He went to London
  + HOME: *I went home*
  + TO + NP: *I went to the cinema*
  + particle: *I went out*
                               Why did you go away?
                               Don't go in now
                               We went back
                               Are you going up/down?

GOING TO   See: Future, Intention

GOOD   Irregular comparison. See under: Comparative forms

GOT   See under: HAVE

HALF   *It's half past three*
                               Give me half of it
                               Give me half a bottle

HAVE
  as full verb
  (= POSSESS):   *I have about $25*
                               Have you a room for one night?
                               Do you have a room for one night?
  (= EAT, DRINK, etc):   *to have (a meal)*
  (with ailments):   *I have (got) a cold*
  as auxiliary: *I have been to Paris*
                                 I have not seen John yet
  + GOT   *We have got a new car*
  + TO (necessity):   *Do I have to leave?*
                                 I have to/don't have to see him
                               We had to/didn't have to wait five minutes

  in present perfect: *I have been to Paris*
                                 I have booked two rooms

HEAR:
  after CAN: *I can hear you*

68

HERE
adv place (stress)ed:

It's here
Here he is

to indicate:

Here it is
Here's the bus

HIGH
with reference to things only:

That's a high mountain
See: LOW

HOME

I go home at six
He is at home

HOPE
+ (THAT):

I hope (that) you can help me

HOW
asking for adv manner:
+ adj with reference to:

How can I do it?

  age:

How old are you?

  cost/price

How much are these shoes?

  distance:

How far/near is it?

  height:

How high is it?

  length:

How long is it?

  quantity:

How much/many do you want?

  size:

How big/small is it?

  temp:

How hot/cold is it?

  weight:

How heavy is it?

Imperative

Look out!
Don't look now!
Be careful!

IN
as adv particle:

Don't go in now

referring to place:

Edinburgh is in Scotland
I work in a shop
I had to stand in the train

referring to time:

I'll see you in July/in 19..
It often rains in (the) winter
I'll see you in two weeks

IN FRONT OF

There's a tree in front of the house

Indefinite article

See: A/An, Zero

Indefinite pronoun

See: SOME compounds

Indirect object

He gave the ticket to my brother
He have me a book

Infinitive
as object: eg:

I want to buy a pair of shoes

expressing purpose: eg:

He came to help me

INSIDE
    as particle: *My car is inside*

Intensifiers   *It's much better*
                                See also under: TOO, VERY

Intention
    with GOING TO: *I'm going to stay here for a week*

Interrogative form
    of auxiliaries/modals: *Is that the right word?*
                                Have you (got) a telephone?
                                Can you speak French?

    with DO/DOES/DID: *Do you like ice-cream?*
                                Does he like ice-cream?
                                Did you see a man with a big suitcase?

    with Question words (WHO and
    WHICH) as subject (no inversion):   *Who told you that?*
                                Which bus goes to Oxford Circus?

    WHO(M)? WHAT? WHICH   *How do you say that in English?*
    WHOSE? HOW? WHEN?   *When will it be ready?*
    WHERE? WHY? (with   *Where did you go (last night)?*
    inversion):   *Where have you been?*
                                What are you going to do tonight?

INTO   *He went into the house*

Intonation
    especially with reference to:
    WH–questions and Yes/No questions
    echoed questions
    questions in statement form
    requests and commands

Invitations   See under: WOULD

Irregular adjectives   See under: Comparative forms

Irregular plurals   See under: Plural nouns

Irregular verbs

The following occur in the *Lexicon*:

be	was	been
break	broke	broken
bring	brought	brought
burn	burnt	burnt
buy	bought	bought
come	came	come
cut	cut	cut
do	did	done
drink	drank	drunk
drive	drove	driven
eat	ate	eaten

70

fall	fell	fallen
get	got	got
give	gave	given
go	went	gone
have	had	had
hear	heard	heard
keep	kept	kept
know	knew	known
learn	learnt	learnt
leave	left	left
lose	lost	lost
make	made	made
mean	meant	meant
pay	paid	paid
put	put	put
read	read	read
say	said	said
see	saw	seen
sell	sold	sold
send	sent	sent
show	showed	shown
sing	sang	sung
sit	sat	sat
speak	spoke	spoken
stand	stood	stood
steal	stole	stolen
take	took	taken
tell	told	told
think	thought	thought
understand	understood	understood
write	wrote	written

IT as subject

It's very good
It's raining
It doesn't matter
It's a quarter past three
It takes five minutes

JUST

I've just seen him

LAST
  as adv:
  in time references:

Peter came last
I saw him last week
Compare: NEXT

LATE

We were too late for the train
He arrived late

Length

How long is it?
The car is thirteen ft long

LET'S
  in suggestions:

Let's go to the cinema

71

LIKE
    after WOULD: *Would you like .. .?*
    as a verb: *I like your brother very much*
                                    I like ice-cream
    + TO-infinitive: *I'd like to sit down now*

LITTLE
    with mass nouns: *I have very little money*

A LITTLE (= A QUANTITY OF):   *Milk? Only a little, please*

Long
    distance: *This road is very long*
    duration: *We had to wait a long time*

LOOK
    as a verb: *Look at his new car*
    + particle: *Look out!*

A LOT OF
    in affirmative statements with
    mass and unit nouns: *I've got a lot of time/books*

LOW
    with reference to things only: *That's a low mountain*
                                  See: HIGH

MAKE
    basic meaning: *She made a new dress*
    + OF: *It's made of wool*

MANY
    as quantifier: *I've got too many*
    in negative statements   *There aren't many taxis in this town*
    with unit nouns: See under: HOW; Present perfect tense

Mass nouns   See under: Nouns

MATTER   *What's the matter?*
                                  It doesn't matter

MAY
    permission: *May I put my coat here?*
    requests: *May I have another cup of tea, please?*

Meals
    no article before meals: *I'd like to wash before dinner*
                                  See: Zero article

Measures/volume   PINT, GALLON as given in the *Lexicon*

Modals   See under: CAN, MAY, WOULD

Months of the year   See under: Dates

MORE
    with mass and unit nouns: *I want more stamps/time*

72

MOST
    with mass and unit nouns:
        Most people like ice-cream
        Most shops are closed on Sundays

Motion
    See under: Prepositions

MUCH
    as adverb:
        Thank you very much
        I like . . . very much
    as quantifier:
        There is too much noise here
        Compare: MANY
    as intensifier:
        This is much better
    in negative statements
    with mass nouns:
        There isn't much sugar
        See under: HOW

Names
    See under: Nouns; Zero article

Nationalities
    As required

NEAR
    as preposition:
        We live near the station
        Compare: FAR FROM

Necessity
    See under: HAVE

Negative form
    of BE/auxiliaries/modals:
        This shirt is not clean
        I haven't seen John yet
        He cannot write English very well
    with DO/DOES/DID:
        We don't live far from the station
        It doesn't matter
        He wanted to leave, but he did not say so

NEVER
    with the present:
        I never play football

NEW
    with reference to things:
        We have got a new car
        See also: OLD; YOUNG

NEXT
    in time references:
        I'll see you next week
    + TO (preposition)
        The garage is next to the hotel

NO
    in negative answers:
        No, thank you
    (= NOT ANY):
        See under: SOME
    NO compounds:
        See under: SOME compounds

NOT
    See under: Interrogative form;
    Negative form

NOT . . . ANY
    See under: SOME

NOT . . . MUCH/MANY
    See under: MUCH; MANY

NOTHING   See under: SOME compounds

NOUNS
  common: A CHAIR, AN ANIMAL, etc: as specified
                                             in *Lexicon*
  compound: See: Compound nouns
  count/countable: A CHAIR, AN ANIMAL, etc: as specified
                                             in *Lexicon*
  mass: SUGAR, COFFEE, etc: as specified in
                                             Lexicon
  a mass or unit: BEER/A BEER, COFFEE/A COFFEE,
                                           etc: as specified in *Lexicon*
  partitive: A PAIR/BOTTLE/PIECE/CUP/glass, etc:
                                           OF: as specified in *Lexicon*
  plural: See under: Plural nouns
  proper   Names of people and places as required
  unit   See: Count/Countable above
                                           See also: A/An; plural nouns; SOME;
                                         THE; Zero article

Number   See: Plural nouns

Numbers   Cardinal and ordinal

OF   See under: Genitive; Prepositions
                                         A GLASS OF WATER: See under:
                                         Nouns: partitive

Offers   See under: CAN, WOULD

OFTEN   *He's often late*

OLD
  as opposite of NEW: *We have got an old car*
  and YOUNG: *I am too old for this*
  comparisons: people and things: *He's/It's older*

ON
  referring to place: *The food was on the table*
  referring to time: *I'll see you on Monday*
                                         There is an early train on Mondays
                                         I was born in London on 26th July 1930

ONCE   *He came once*
                                         See also: A/An

ONE
  as pronoun/propword: *May I have the red one, please?*
  distinguishing from A/An: *Have you a room for one night?*
  in place of A/An + Unit: *Can you show me another one?*

ONLY
  positions: *Milk? Only a little, please*

OR
  joining words or phrases: *It's black or white*
  joining clauses: *We can go to the beach or stay at home*

Ordinal numbers   Up to two digits; eg 20th, 21st, 22nd, 23rd,
                                           24th etc.

OTHER
  (= ALTERNATIVE):   *Give me the other book*

OUT
  as particle: *We walked out*

OUT OF   *He came out of the house*

OUTSIDE
  as particle: *My wife is outside*

Participle   See: Past participle, Present participle

Particle   See: Adverbial particle; Adverbial; trans-
                                           posable particle

Partitive   See under: Nouns, partitive

PAST
  as preposition: *It's a quarter-past three*

Past participle
  after HAVE in Present
perfect: *I have broken my glasses*
  used adjectivally: *The dog is dead*
                                           The door is closed

Past tense
  with irregular verbs: See: Irregular verbs
  with regular verbs: See: Regular verbs
  with exact time reference: *Where did you go last night?*

Period of time   See under: FOR, SINCE

Permission   See under: CAN, MAY

Personal pronouns   See under: Pronouns

Phrasal verbs
  intransitive: eg: *Sit down/Wake up*
  transitive: eg: *Put on your coat*
                                           Put your coat on
                                           Put it on

Plural nouns
  Form and spelling:
  + -s: CARS, FRIENDS
  + -es: GLASSES, WATCHES
  consonant -y to -ies: FACTORIES

-fe to -ves:	KNIVES, WIVES
irregular:	CHILDREN, FEET, MEN, TEETH, WOMEN
used only as plural:	GLASSES, PEOPLE
used only as singular:	LUGGAGE, NEWS, SUGAR, COFFEE
pronunciation:	
/s/ after 'k', 'p', 't'	SOCKS, CUPS, ADULTS
/z/:	CARS, DOGS, LETTERS
/iz/:	HOUSES, WATCHES

Point
  in space: See under: Adverbial, place, Prepositions

  of time: See under: Adverbial, time, Prepositions; AT; IN; ON; SINCE

Possession   See under: HAVE

Possessive   See under: Pronouns; Genitive

Predicative   See under: Adjectives

Prepositions   See: ABOUT, AGAINST, AT, BEHIND, BETWEEN, DOWN, FOR, FROM, IN, INSIDE, INTO, NEXT TO, ON, OUT OF, OUTSIDE, SINCE, THROUGH, TO, UP, WITH

after verb:	See under: Verbs
at the end of a question:	*Where are you from?*
of motion:	TO, FROM, etc
of position:	IN, AT, etc
of time:	IN, AT, etc

Present continuous tense   See: Present progressive tense

Present participle
  in progressive aspect: *It's raining*

Present perfect tense
BEEN and GONE:	*He's gone to Paris*
	He's been to Paris
no time reference:	*The weather has changed*
repeated actions:	*I've seen him twice/many times*
with JUST:	*I've just seen him*
with NOT . . . YET/ALREADY:	*I have not seen John yet*
	I have already done it
with SINCE + exact time reference	*I've been here since Thursday*
with FOR + a period of time:	*I've been here for two hours*

Present progressive tense
current action:	*Are you going up?*
	I am going down

76

Present simple tense habitual:	*This train goes to London* *I always listen to the news*
with stative verbs:	*I want a soft pillow* *cf.* KNOW, LIKE, LIVE, MEAN, UNDERSTAND
Progressive aspect	See under: Present progressive tense
Prohibition	See: DO/DID: in imperatives (negative)
Pronouns indefinite:	See under: SOME, SOME compounds
personal subject:	I, we, he, she, it, they, you
object:	me, us, him, her, it, them, you
possessive adjectives and pronouns:	my, mine; our, ours; his, his; her, hers; its, its; your, yours; their, theirs
Proper nouns	See under: Nouns
Purpose	See under: Clauses, purpose
PUT ON	*Put on your hat* *Put your hat on* *Put it on*
Quantifiers/Determiners:	See under: ALL; A LOT OF; SOME; MANY; MUCH; ENOUGH; LITTLE; FEW; HALF; NOUNS partitive

Quantity
  of mass:
	How much do you want?
	I want a pound (lb)/a kilo (kg)
	    a little

of units:	*How many do you want?*
	I want five
	    two pounds (lbs)/kilos (kgs)
	    a few
	See under: HOW; MANY; MUCH; Quantifiers: SOME

Questions	See: Interrogative form; Prepositions
Reason	See under: Clauses, cause/reason
Regular verbs + -d, + -ed /d/: eg:	Verbs as given in *Lexicon* ARRIVED, CLEARED
+ -ed /t/: eg:	WASHED
+ -ed /id/ after /t/, /d/: eg:	WAITED
+ -ied /aid/ or /i:d/ in place of consonant + -y: eg:	TRIED
Requests	See under: MAY, CAN

RIGHT
  after **BE**:   *Is that the right word?*

ROUND
  as adj: *It's round*

SAME   *This is the same*
                                                    They came home at the same time
                                                    This coat is the same size as that
                                                    See: **DIFFERENT**

SEE
  after **CAN**:   *I can see you*
  (=**MEET**):   *I haven't seen John yet*

SEND   *Send it to me*
                                                    See under: Direct object

Shape   *It's round/square, etc*

SHORT
  as adj opposite of **LONG**:   *I want a short coat*
  duration: *We waited a short time*

Short answers, eg
  adj complement: *What colour is it? Black*
  adv place/prep phrase: *Where is he? In the garden*
  adv time: *When will he be here? On Monday*
  NP object: *What's he reading? A book*
  Yes/No tag answers: *Is he here: Yes, he is/No, he isn't*

SHOW   *Show it to me*
                                                    See under: Direct object

Simple past tense   See: Past tense

Simple present tense   See: Present simple tense

Simple sentences
  not more than two complements: *Bring me some water*
                                                    I'd like to take this with me

SINCE
  + exact time reference: *I've been here since Thursday*
                                                    I haven't seen him since Monday

Size   *How big is it?*
                                                    It's very big
                                                    Size 41 please
                                                    See under: **HOW**

SO
  (=**THEREFORE**):   *He didn't arrive so I left*
  after **THINK**:   *I think so*

SOME, ANY, NO + mass/plural units
  SOME
  affirmative: *Bring me some water*
                                          I want to buy some stamps

  ANY
  negatives: *I want a new car, but I have not got any money*
                                          I haven't got any stamps
  questions: *Have you got any sugar/stamps?*
  NO
  + noun (= NOT ANY):   *I've got no sugar/stamps*

SOME–/ANY/–NO–/compounds: SOMETHING
                                          ANYTHING
                                          NOTHING

SOME–/ANY–/NO– compounds follow basic SOME/ANY/NO pattern

SOMETIMES   *He's sometimes late*

SOON
  with future reference: *I'll see you soon*

SORRY
  to apologize: *I'm sorry*

SPEAK
  a language: *Can you speak French?*

Spelling   See under: Plural nouns; Regular verbs

Stative verbs   See under: Present simple tense: stative
                                          verbs

STILL
  to emphasize continuity: *He is still working*

STOP   *The car stopped in front of a garage*

Subordinating conjunctions   BECAUSE, THAT, TO + inf

Suggestions   *Let's . . .*

Tags   See under: Short answers

TAKE   *How long does it take?*
                                          It takes five minutes (by taxi)

TELL
  + ABOUT: *Tell me about your work*

Temperature   *How hot/cold is it?*

Tenses   See under: Future; Present; Past

THAN   See under: Comparisons

THAT   See under: Clauses; Demonstrative

THE
  definite article: *May I have the red one, please?*
  singular unit: *The dog was under the table*
  plural units: *The dogs were under the table*
  mass noun: *The food was on the table*
  referring to one only: *We were too late for the train*
  referring to place: *We buy our vegetables at the market*
                                 We live near the station

THEN
  (= AT THE TIME):   *I'll see you then*
  (= AFTER THAT):   *First we went to London, then we went to Paris*

THERE
  adv place (stressed):   *It's there!*
                                 There he is!
  existential (unstressed):   *There's a man outside*
                                 There was nothing there

THESE   See under: Demonstratives

THINK
  + SO:
  + (THAT):   *I think so/I don't think so*
                                 I think (that) you are ill
                                 See under: VERB + THAT

THIS   See under: Demonstratives

THOSE   See under: Demonstratives

THROUGH   *He went through the centre of the town*

TILL   *I'll be here till six o'clock*

Time
  telling the time including
  reference to the 24 hour clock
  of day/greetings etc: THIS MORNING, etc
                                 GOOD MORNING, etc
  point of time: See under: Adverbial, of time; AT; IN;
                                 ON

Titles
  as in: *Mr, Mrs, Miss*

TO
  as preposition: *This train goes to London*
  in infinitive constructions: *I want to see him*
                                 See under: Verbs
  purpose: *He came to help me*

TOO
  (= ALSO):   *John is going to come too*
  as intensifier (= EXCESSIVELY):   *This blanket is too heavy*
                                 See: VERY

Transitive verb	See under: Verb
Uncountable noun	See under: Nouns
UP	
as particle:	*I woke up at six*
as preposition:	*Are you going up?*
VERB	See under: BE, DO, HAVE (auxiliaries); Irregular; Phrasal; Regular; Stative (see Present simple); Tense (under Present; Past)
+ TO:	Some verbs from the *Lexicon* that will combine with TO: LIKE, WANT
+ THAT:	Some verbs from the *Lexicon* that will combine with THAT: THINK, HOPE
+ Preposition:	Prepositions that will combine with some of the verbs in the *Lexicon*: GET UP, LEAVE FROM, LISTEN TO, LOOK AT, SIT DOWN, WAIT FOR
Verb used intransitively:	*It's raining*
	Don't look now!
Verb used transitively:	*I always listen to the news*
	I don't play football
VERY	
as intensifier:	*He's very old*
	See: TOO
WANT	*I want a short coat*
	See under: Present simple tense, stative verbs
WANT TO	*He wanted to leave, but he did not say so*
	See under: Verbs TO infinitive
WELL	
as adverbial of manner:	*He cannot write English very well*
WHAT	
in WH– questions:	See under: Interrogative form
WHEN	
in WH– questions:	See under: Interrogative form
WHERE	
in WH– questions:	See under: Interrogative form
WHICH	
in WH–questions:	See under: Interrogative form
WHO	
in WH– questions:	See under: Interrogative form

81

WHO(M) in WH– questions	See under: Interrogative form
WHOSE in WH– questions:	See under: Interrogative form
WILL plain future:	*When will it be ready?*
WITH (=ACCOMPANYING; IN THE COMPANY OF): instrumental: possession:	*We are going to take John with us* *You can open the door with this key* *Did you see a man with a big suitcase?*
WITHOUT (=NOT ACCOMPANYING): instrumental: not possessing:	*We cannot go without you* *You can't open the door without this key* *Don't go there without your passport*
WOOL	*This dress is made of wool*
WOULD in offers, invitations:	*Would you like a cup of coffee?* *Would you like to go out tonight?*
Word order basic statement patterns:	(Time)/Subject/Verb/Object/Manner/Place/(Tim For changes from this pattern see: Interrogative form:
WRONG after BE:	*That word is wrong* *You're wrong*
Years spoken convention: eg: written convention, eg:	*nineteen hundred, nineteen one, nineteen two, etc* *1900, 1901, 1902, etc*
Yes/No questions: tags:	See under: Interrogative form See under: Short answers
YET in negatives: in questions:	*He hasn't come yet* *Has he come yet?* See: ALREADY; Present perfect tense
YOU (=ONE)	*How do you say that in English?*
YOUNG with reference to people:	 *He is very young*

82

Zero article
no article before
a place or means of
transport as defined by its
purpose: *by air, train, car, etc*
                                      go home

meals: *I'd like to wash before dinner*
mass nouns: *May I have another cup of tea, please?*
personal pronouns: *That's my book. It's mine*
plural units: *I go out with friends*
topographical names; names   *Edinburgh is in Scotland*
of people; titles; languages;   *I live at number 15 Bridge Street*
proper nouns: *John came first*
                                      He cannot write English very well
                                      Mr/Mrs/Miss

APPENDIX

SOME METHODOLOGICAL IMPLICATIONS OF WAYSTAGE AND THRESHOLD LEVELS

L G Alexander

1. Introductory remarks

Waystage and *Threshold Level* specifications have profound implications for language course design and, by extension, for language teaching and learning. For this reason the term, 'methodology', must be taken to refer both to course design and to actual teaching and learning. While we must accept without question that there is no single 'best method', we must also allow that not all methods are of equal value. There are many roads to Rome, but some are more direct than others and quite a number never arrive at all. When discussing methodology, our main concern must be cost effectiveness. The difficulty of learning a language should not be underestimated and there are no short cuts, but this realization should never inhibit us from constantly seeking more effective (and therefore less time-consuming) ways of fulfilling this formidable undertaking. It is precisely this search that has led to the formulation of *Waystage* and *Threshold Level* specifications.

It is worth beginning any discussion of methodology with a broad definition of the term 'language course'. It is easier to say what a course is not than what it is: *Waystage* and *Threshold Level* specifications, for instance, are not a language course; nor is any kind of syllabus; nor is a grammar book or a dictionary. All of these present some of the raw facts of language. A course differs from specifications and inventories in that it constitutes an attempt to process the raw facts of a language into an organized system which will facilitate its acquisition. That is why it is rarely possible to learn a language directly from a grammar book or a dictionary. At best, a language course can only lubricate the process of acquisition so that learning is motivated, enjoyable and effective. We must assume that most general courses will set out to communicate the four skills of understanding, speaking, reading and writing, though the degree to which each of these is developed may vary enormously. The challenge to the course designer is to create an integrated and above all teachable system which will develop these skills; the challenge to the teacher is to interpret the system creatively and adapt it to suit the needs of his class in order to communicate the four skills; the challenge to the learner is to acquire these skills to the limit of his potential in the time available.

Broadly speaking, course design can be considered under three headings: *Why? What?* and *How?*

Why? refers to the establishment of priorities: Why am I going to do this and not that? We can only arrive at these priorities after we have taken into account all the *constraints* which will influence our decision. *What?* refers to *overall framework:* What am I going to teach? and *How?* refers to *method.* These three headings, *Constraints, Overall Framework*, and *Method* can provide a useful schema for discussion of the methodological implications of *Waystage and Threshold Level* specifications.

2. Constraints (Why?)

In the *Waystage* introduction the communication need of the learner is established as an important constraint. In the context of course design as a whole, this must be seen as one of a large number of possible limitations which are too numerous to list exhaustively. But here, in random order, are some of the most important ones:

Age range:
How old are the learners? Are they all the same age? Are there different age groups in the same class?

Motivation:
Why are they learning language? Is it to achieve something highly specific, like passing an examination or doing a job? Or is it for some general reason: eg to occupy their spare time, or because the educational system requires it? Do they want to integrate with a foreign language community or not? Are they attending classes of their own volition or are they a 'captive audience'?

Washback:
To what extent does an external syllabus or examination influence the teaching/learning set-up? Is this influence desirable? If it is undesirable, can it be modified or altered, or does it have to be endured?

Student background:
Do the learners have roughly the same educational background or not? How do they vary in terms of individual ability? Are they streamed into ability groups? What is their past learning history: are they zero beginners or false beginners?

Teacher background:
How fluent is the teacher's command of the language he is teaching? How much training has he had? How many opportunities does he have for re-training? How did the teacher acquire command of the foreign language he is teaching? How does the teacher's learning experience influence his choice of materials?

Opportunity:
Will the learners put the foreign language to immediate use while they are still learning? Will they hope to put the language to use after a course of study? Are they unlikely to have any opportunity to use the foreign language in the foreseeable future?

Materials:
Does the teacher have freedom of choice, or does he have to use what is available? What resources are there in terms of hardware (tape recorders, overhead projectors, etc) or software (tapes, slides, etc)?

Time (duration):
How much time is allocated to language study? Is it a short-term course (eg six weeks) or a long-term course (eg up to eight years)? What is the total number of teaching/learning hours available? How much extra time can be assumed for homework? How much time has to be realistically written off for holidays, etc?

Time (frequency):
How is the time distributed: eg how many lessons are there per week and how long is each lesson?

Physical:
How many students are there in a class? What are the class conditions? Is there a lot of outside noise? Is the classroom

| | comfortable (too hot, cold, etc)? |
| Day-to-day: | At what time of the day are lessons held: eg early in the day or after the students have done a full day's work, etc? How many other commitments (work, study, etc) has the learner got? How many hours per day is the teacher expected to teach – including extra-institutional work? |

Over and above these factors, there are publishing constraints to the extent that course designers have to develop materials within a limited number of pages and there are the constraints imposed by page layout and design. The likely cost of the end-product to the consumer may seriously affect methodological decisions (determining such questions as eg the number of tapes to be made available) and may take priority over everything else.

Waystage and *Threshold Level* specifications indicate for a defined public what has to be taught if effective communication is to be achieved. The problem for the course designer and the teacher is how to manipulate this information, given the constraints which must be taken into account. While it is possible to define a large target audience which shares a number of these constraints, there will always be variations and conflicts even within quite small groups of learners. Teacher and learner must resolve their conflicts together by constantly modifying materials and techniques and by constantly responding imaginatively and intelligently to an ever-changing situation.

3. Overall framework (What?)

In *Waystage* and *Threshold Level* specifications the principle of selection has already been applied: *what* we have to teach is clearly defined, but, drawing on this definition, the individual user must decide on his own priorities and must develop his own framework for a course, while at the same time ensuring that the specifications are adequately covered. The elementary nature of the utterances we are trying to teach at zero and near-zero should not lull us into thinking that a rudimentary framework will provide an adequate vehicle: quite the contrary. The simpler the utterances to be taught, the more complex the framework that will be required to carry them.

3.1 *Orthodox specifications compared with* Waystage *and* Threshold Level

Orthodox specifications (eg as often defined by Ministries of Education and published as syllabuses in different parts of the world) usually consist of two inventories: one grammatical and the other lexical. The implication is that learning a language involves the mastery of a grammatical system and the concurrent acquisition of a serviceable 'minimum adequate' vocabulary. *Waystage* and *Threshold Level* specifications, by comparison, bring together a number of different factors which are considered indispensable for verbal communication. As is clearly indicated (see *Waystage* introduction) the objectives are behavioural (note that this term has nothing to do with behaviouristic stimulus/response language teaching techniques). Verbal communication is seen to be highly complex (compared with the components of the orthodox syllabus) for it is recognized that not only are there 'grammatical rules' but rules which are part of the system of social behaviour (which we may think of as 'rules for use'): what we say and how we say it depends on such factors as what the speakers

87

want to *do* through language, what their relationship is, what the setting is and so on. In *Waystage* and *Threshold Level* specifications the grammatical and lexical components remain limited, but they are seen as only a small part of the total system of language behaviour: both sets of specifications set out to identify and describe many of the different factors which influence verbal communication.

Of course, the very best language courses based on orthodox specifications set out to teach the skills of understanding, speaking, reading and writing and to that extent they are likely to have much in common with materials based on a functional/notional approach. Furthermore, the results from teaching a good conventional course may not necessarily differ very much from those that might be obtained from a good functional/notional course.

However, *Waystage* and *Threshold Level* specifications are certain to give rise to a different kind of framework as a basis for course construction because the starting point stems from an analysis of language needs in communicative rather than grammatical terms. In a conventional course, grammatical items are often taught because they are considered important in themselves. By comparison, the main criterion for choosing and teaching an item in a functional/notional approach can only be its communicative validity. In this discussion it is therefore reasonable to consider (together with their advantages and shortcomings) the following:

The structural framework
The situational application of the structural framework
Possible alternative frameworks
The situational application of a functional/notional approach.

3.2 The structural framework

With the development of audio-visual and audio-lingual courses from the mid 1950s onwards, there has been a move away from formal grammar lessons and the presentation of complete paradigms. Courses have been increasingly based on graded sequences of structures, a form of organization which is known as 'structural grading'. In such an approach the steps are carefully ordered in terms of apparent increasing difficulty. Teachers using such materials have been conditioned to accept (but not altogether unquestioningly) certain prescribed sequences. Although these are arrived at intuitively, there is sufficient agreement in most language courses to allow us to refer to 'structural grading' as if it were some kind of objective system. For instance, most English courses begin with *be + noun/adjective* combinations, proceeding to *have/have got + noun/adjective* combinations and then on to the present continuous, the simple present, the simple past, the present perfect, and so on. In various parts of the world this progression is often reinforced by ministerial syllabuses in which these sequences are outlined fairly precisely and prescribed textbooks are usually required to conform to the syllabus. The result (in textbook terms) is a logico-grammatical framework of interrelated pattern sequences. When one sequence is played out, a new one is taken up until an extensive area of language has been covered. The assumption always is that it is easier to teach *I am tired* than *I might have been able to see you earlier if you had given me a ring*; structural grading can be simply described as the steps which link these two poles.

The framework described is linear. But cyclical variations are also possible. In a cyclical structural framework, a particular area of difficulty may be deliberately

re-introduced at different intervals (say, every twenty lessons) so that a little more information is added each time. Thus, for example, the present perfect may first be introduced in the form *have been*, then later in conjunction with *just, already*, and *yet*, then again in conjunction with *since* and *for*; at an even later stage the student may be introduced to the present perfect continuous. The system of structural grading has been applied with increasing sophistication and it is not unusual to find beginners' courses which are ordered in a linear fashion, followed by pre-intermediate and intermediate courses which are ordered in a cyclical fashion.

The system has led to greater efficiency in the classroom and is a considerable improvement on the formal presentation of paradigms. However, constant application has brought many weaknesses to light and this has provided some of the impetus for the development of alternative functional/notional syllabuses. The main weaknesses can be described as follows:

a. The student cannot always see the practical application of what he is learning to real life. While focus on the grammar can produce reasonable utterances like *There is a glass on the table*, it can (and frequently does) give rise to patent absurdities, such as *There is a green book behind your head*. In the case of the adult student, in particular this can only set up a resistance to learning in the classroom. The learner, who may have been motivated to attend classes for wholly practical reasons, can easily find himself producing utterances which will be far removed from what he really wants to say.

b. Structural grading attempts to communicate a large part of the grammatical system, often giving as much emphasis to low frequency items as to high frequency ones. Though it is obviously based on a selection of language, it aims at completeness. Consequently, the build-up is slow. The student rarely reaches the past tense by the end of Book One, so that after a year's study he may still be unable to formulate a simple but obviously useful statement like *I went to the cinema last night*. On the other hand, he may have put a good deal of effort into learning and practising the various uses of the impersonal pronoun *its* 'for the sake of completeness'.

c. The definition of what is 'easy' and 'difficult' is usually made wholly in terms of structural progression. Thus a student may be taught to say *I want a cup of coffee* simply because the focus in that particular lesson happens to be on the simple present with stative verbs, but he is denied access to *I'd like a cup of coffee* because the implied use of the subjunctive *would* is arbitrarily defined as 'too difficult at this stage'. As a result, the student is not generally made aware of the stylistic register and the kind of language that is really appropriate to any given situations.

3.3 The situational application of the structural framework

The system of structural grading has been widely applied through the presentation of 'situations', an approach that has come to be referred to loosely as 'situational teaching'. In fact, this term covers a variety of approaches which can be described as follows:

Classroom situational
Centre interest situational
Structurally-controlled situational
Story-line situational.

3.3.1 Classroom situational

This approach takes the classroom situation as the basis for language acquisition and is an extremely common way of beginning a language. It usually takes the form of identifying the objects in the classroom and naming them and makes extensive use of classroom props for a variety of activities. The approach barely merits the term *situational* at all, for it has little to do with ordinary human situations. While the classroom *can* be exploited in positive and useful ways, it is, by definition, an extremely limited environment. It is perhaps inevitable that it often encourages a totally absurd use of language (*Is this a pen? Have you got a nose? Are you a boy? How many ears have you got? Stand up. Go to the door. What are you doing? – I am going to the door* etc). This kind of language is often reflected in textbooks at the beginners' level and is widely taught. More than any other single factor, it probably accounts for loss of motivation to learn a language and for early drop-out (in the case of non-captive student audiences).

3.3.2 Centre of interest situational

In this form of organization the course designer attempts to predict the kinds of situation the student might encounter in real life and seeks to prepare him for them, taking such obvious themes as *the post office, the Customs,* etc. The situations may or may not be structurally graded depending on the framework the course designer has adopted. Language study is usually derived from each situation. While dialogues based on well-selected centres of interest can obviously have a practical value in that they provide a lot of useful language, they are presented on the demonstrably false assumption that the student will be able to function in the same way when he finds himself in similar circumstances. It is naive to suppose that we can predict precisely what people will say in such situations; nor is there any way in which the student can learn to cope with the unexpected. Furthermore, although a great many such situations may look different on the surface (eg *the restaurant* may seem to be very remote from *buying tickets*), in fact they often give rise to the same kind of language. This suggests we should be looking for communicative features which many such situations share rather than treating each one as if it were linguistically discrete and somehow unique.

3.3.3 Structurally-controlled situational

This approach takes a structure or a set of structures out of the graded sequence as its starting point, rather than a *centre of interest*. The structure is then 'situationalized' or – to use the accepted term – *contextualized*. From the course designer's point of view, the situation itself is relatively unimportant: it is the structure that takes precedence over everything else and the main purpose of the situation is to illustrate a grammatical point. Thus, for example, if the course designer wants to illustrate the use of *have been to* . . . he will write a situation round this structure, trying as far as possible to make the use of the form sound inevitable and correct. This approach has the advantage that the student is exposed to only a small amount of new language at any one time. However, the situations tend to be random and inconsequential. Furthermore, in real life, situations never develop within the confines of carefully pre-selected structural items.

3.3.4 Story-line situational

Both the centre of interest approach and the structurally-controlled situational approach may have some kind of story-line superimposed on them. A particular unifying theme, involving a character or characters, is set up at the beginning of the course and then developed through a series of episodes, which (in the case of zero beginners' courses) are usually unconnected. The unifying theme may concern a family, or (say) a protagonist who has just arrived in a foreign country and whose subsequent stay is carefully plotted.

Story-lines can be suitable in children's beginners' (up to the age of 12+) or in multi-media courses aimed at adults where thematic continuity is paramount. In the case of children, they provide a useful focal point; in the case of adult multi-media courses, they may have an entertainment value. However, the story-line generally palls in the case of adult zero beginners' textbooks, the antics of the characters becoming increasingly irrelevant to the needs of the learner as the course progresses. The acute linguistic restrictions make it impossible to present anything but the most mundane situations, the development of the story-line is extremely slow and ponderous; few – if any – course designers have the necessary literary skills to create and sustain a story-line which will really appeal to an adult. While the presentation may be attractive in the first book, it merely becomes irritating when the student has got beyond the elementary level.

3.4 Possible alternative frameworks

The behavioural (rather than grammatical) emphasis of *Waystage* and *Threshold Level* specifications provides us with the means of developing alternative frameworks, but it will be a long time before we have sufficient variety of such forms of organization to be able to assess their relative efficacy. At the time of writing the models available remain largely theoretical and, particularly in the case of zero beginners' courses, pose a formidable challenge to course designers. Possible forms of organization might be:

A functional framework
A structural/functional framework
A functional/structural framework
Thematic areas.

3.4.1 A functional framework

While it is theoretically possible to conceive of a framework which consists wholly of *language acts*, it seems unlikely that such a model could have more than a limited application (in phrase books for instance). A framework which took functions like, identifying, reporting, correcting, asking, expressing agreement and disagreement, etc as its starting point and consciously ignored the grammatical implications of these acts would be extremely deficient, for the student also needs to operate the grammatical system to communicate adequately. Ultimately, we cannot ignore the need to master grammatical paradigms if fluency is to be achieved. Furthermore, there are dangers implicit in functional labelling, exponents of functions are not necessarily discrete. For example, *It's hot* (with subtle variations in intonation) can be

91

an exponent of describing, complaining, reporting, explaining, correcting, denying, agreeing, disagreeing, and so on. It would be misleading to assume that the student could learn a codified set of exponents for particular functions which would serve in all circumstances.

It should also be noted that the exponents of some functions are merely phrases which can be learnt by heart (eg *Cheers!*, the exponent of 'proposing a toast', is a fixed expression) while other functions relate to total grammatical systems and require an enormous amount of time and effort to master (eg the exponents of 'Asking'). This distinction between fixed phrases and 'grammatical system' is indicated in *Waystage*: the former exponents being underscored with a broken line. There are also other exponents which are part of the grammatical system but which we may wish to teach early as fixed phrases: for instance, we may wish to teach *I'd like* . . . early but not all its paradigms. Such exponents are also indicated with a broken line in the *Waystage* inventories.

3.4.2 A structural/functional framework

The biggest challenge facing course designers is to devise a framework which makes full use of the communicative potential of a functional/notional approach while at the same time enabling the learner to master and operate the grammatical system.
One possible model might involve setting out with grammatical objectives which are interpreted behaviourally: the emphasis being on the *function* the grammar represents, not just the grammar itself. In such an approach it might be possible to retain a structurally graded sequence, but to accrue to it ungraded-but-semantically-related patterns. Thus, if the first lesson were concerned with 'personal identification' (in relation to names and jobs) it would be possible to teach *What's your name?* (structurally graded) and *What do you do? (for a living)?* (structurally ungraded) in the same lesson. The low frequency and stylistically clumsy *What are you?* (which strict structural grading would demand) would not be taught at all. *What do you do?* (which would be delayed in a rigidly graded course until the simple present had been reached) would be taught in preference because this is the stylistically acceptable norm when considering an objective of this kind.

A factor any course designer using this model would have to guard against is the possibility that orthodox structural grading might still tend to dominate. A truly communicative approach (implying as it does diversity of utterance) may make such an orderly progression difficult. It could be argued that if the control system is too orderly, the communicative objectives would take second place or get lost altogether.

3.4.3 A functional/structural framework

This might involve setting out with behavioural objectives and deriving language practice from them. Teaching people how to do things would take precedence over the grammar, but the grammatical components of each communicative undertaking would be practised intensively. The student would learn 'a bit of everything at the same time'. How well course designers, teachers and students will be able to cope with a consciously or apparently unsystematic acquisition of grammar remains to be seen. The approach may, nonetheless, lead to interesting developments.

92

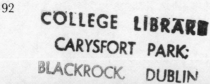

3.4.4 Thematic areas

Another possible framework might be to deal with a particular *thematic area* over a number of lessons. For example 'Finding the way' might be considered a thematic area of this kind. In this approach the student would be carefully guided through the steps involved in this particular area. Such a sequence would cover the use of a few ordinal numbers; distinguishing between left and right with reference to simple maps (*The first turning on the left, The second turning on the right* etc); giving and understanding simple directions to places (*Where's the nearest bank? It's down the first street on the left*); handling prepositions (*It's opposite, near, next to* etc); handling the imperative (*Take the first turning . . . Go down . . .*); coping with landmarks (*Go down this street until you come to a cinema*); learning to cope with indoor and outdoor locations; coping with directions as a pedestrian or as a motorist; coping with modes of transport and distances. Thus the student would be actively taught how to eg find his way from analysis of what 'finding the way' actively involves. Within such a sequence some of the grammatical components have to be actively assimilated (eg prepositional relationship) while others (connective like *until you come to . . .*) would be learnt as fixed phrases. The problem in this approach is to define the thematic areas. There may also be a danger that in isolating particular areas we fail to get continuity in the course as a whole.

The system of grading can still be implemented in a functional/notional framework. For instance, it might be possible to devise a cyclical approach which allows the learner to acquire simple utterances first and more complex ones at a later stage. Thus, for example, when learning how to ask for permission, the learner can set out with a relatively simple and straightforward form like *Can I (borrow your umbrella) please?* and through a process of recycling eventually learns to cope with a really complex request for permission like eg *I hope you don't mind my asking, but could I possibly (borrow your umbrella) please?* However, grading in a functional/notional approach can be an altogether different kind of undertaking as will be seen in paragraph 3.5.4.

3.5 The situational application of a functional/notional approach

In the situational application of the structural framework (3.3) such considerations as settings, or roles were seen to be of little consequence, the main concern being to present a structure and/or a particular centre of interest. In a functional/notional approach, 'situational teaching' cannot be so narrowly defined and takes on an altogether different meaning: it is not merely a presentation device for achieving a limited objective, but describes the sum total of all the aspects of communication which occur within any given context. It is used to cover not only grammar and lexis, but functions, notions and their exponents, settings and topics, social and psychological roles, and style and range of expression. *Waystage* and *Threshold Level* specifications fully indicate the major factors that come into play in a situation.

3.5.1 Functions, notions and their exponents

Waystage and *Threshold Level* concentrate on functions with a wide operational force: that is those which can recur in a large number of different situations. Thus, for example, 'expressing preference' can figure in any number of different situational contexts: eg shopping, eating out, hotels, travel, etc. This realization emphasizes the undesirability of presenting different centres of interest as if they were linguistically

93

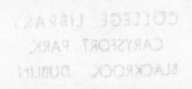

discrete from each other (see 3.3.2). A functional/notional awareness makes it possible for the student to realize than an utterance which applies in one situation can arise equally well in another (see *Waystage* introduction). Language functions may apply to a wide variety of topics and events. What varies is the choice of specific notions which is determined by each topic. For example:

Language function and general notion	Specific notion	Topic
	size 14	(shopping)
I'd like	a steak	(restaurant)
	a double room	(hotel)
	a return ticket	(travel)

3.5.2 Settings and topics

Two aspects can often be discerned in any setting: the *concrete* and the *general*. The concrete aspect can actually influence and even determine the choice of items the speaker will use. Thus, a ticket office, a restaurant, or a hotel reception desk can be defined as concrete in particular circumstances. The general aspect, on the other hand, does not necessarily influence the choice of items the speakers will use: eg a beach, a bus stop, or a dinner table can provide a background for an open-ended conversation or argument. A single setting may be at one and the same time concrete and general. For example, a restaurant can influence the choice of items the speakers will use when they are ordering food etc and at the same time provide a background for the open-ended discussion of a topic. In some settings, the concrete element tends to predominate and open-ended conversation is unlikely (eg a theatre box office); in others the open-ended element predominates (eg a beach).

This distinction is important because the concrete aspect of a setting can lead to a *transaction*. A transaction can be rapidly identified because the language events that will take place are predictable with reasonable accuracy (excluding, of course, the incidence of the unexpected). For example, a group of people may enter a restaurant; they will be told by eg a waiter if the restaurant is full; otherwise they will be asked how many people they want a table for; they will be conducted to a table; then they will be brought a menu; then the waiter will return to take their order, and so on. Much of the language that will be used can be predicted fairly accurately. This kind of *transaction* must be distinguished from the open-ended discussion of a topic:

concrete aspect ⟶ transaction

general aspect ⟶ open-ended
conversation or
argument

The relevance of this distinction to language teaching will be immediately apparent. In teaching 'conversation', we have to distinguish between transactions (the steps of which are to some extent foreseeable and therefore relatively easier to teach) and open-ended conversation and argument (the direction of which is not foreseeable). A transaction can be reduced to an algorithmic model indicating the predictable sequence of events. Such a model is known as a *praxeogram*. The transactional praxeogram is not only relevant to the general learner but also to the specialized

94

learner who is not concerned with acquiring language but with performing efficiently a well-defined task which involves limited use of language: eg operating a machine, serving in a restaurant, etc. A transaction can differ from a centre of interest (described earlier, 3.3.2) because it is concerned only with a narrowly defined sequence of events, not something more general like 'the post office', or 'the restaurant'.

Settings which act really as a backdrop obviously play a less important role in an open-ended conversation or argument. We should also note that a general conversation can be merely an exchange of information or shift rapidly into argument. For instance, from a straight exchange about eg today's weather, we may move directly into an argument involving disagreement about the state of the weather yesterday, last week or last year.

3.5.3 Social, sexual and psychological roles

The relationship between the speakers and their attitudes to each other greatly affects the choice of items and must be clearly established in all situations. It can matter greatly whether the speakers are friends or strangers, male or female, officials or shop assistants, old or young, etc. And this awareness must be built into situations even at *Waystage* to prevent the learner from making social blunders and enable him to handle even simple forms with some degree of subtlety.

3.5.4 Style and range

How the speakers will address each other will be a direct by-product of their social and psychological roles. Speakers may adopt formal or informal styles depending on their relationship and they may express themselves in a variety of ways. This 'variety of ways' we can think of in terms of a 'cline' which can range between extremes like the following: certain/tentative/uncertain or positive/speculative/unpositive. The following three statements will provide an elementary example of what is meant by range:

> *He's 24 years old.* (positive)
> *He may be about 24 years old.* (tentative)
> *I'm not sure how old he is.* (unpositive/uncertain)

Questions of style and range play an important role in distinguishing between lower and higher levels of linguistic ability. At *Waystage* the learners' resources will, of course, be extremely limited.

3.5.5 Grading

In a structural framework, grading is confined narrowly to structures and vocabulary (*see* 3.2). We have also seen how, in turn, it might be possible to grade functions (*see* 3.4.4). However, an even broader application of grading can be made in the situational realization of a functional/notional approach: complete situations can be graded in order of increasing difficulty and complexity. *Waystage* as a whole can be seen as a graded component of the language learning objective; *Threshold Level* can be seen as the next step and so on. Perhaps an example of the way students can learn to handle situations of increasing complexity will make the application of this clear.

Let us suppose that at various stages in a beginners' course, students learn how to describe people in terms of appearance, character, age and skills; suppose they learn to make comparisons and express likes and dislikes. What the students are learning to do can be applied in situations of increasing complexity. For example, early in the course the students may role play an interview situation in which Student A takes the part of the prospective employer and interviews Student B, the prospective employee by asking him questions. At a later stage in the course the interview situation can develop into a more complex role play activity consisting of four main situations:

1. Students A and B (prospective employers) interview Student C (prospective employee) and ask him questions.
2. Student C leaves the room and Students A and B talk about his suitability for the job.
3. Student D (the next prospective employee) is interviewed by Students A and B.
4. Student D leaves the room and Students A and B compare the suitability of Students C and D for the job.

Such a situation can be re-introduced a number of times even to a very advanced level with increasing demands being made on the participants. The principle of grading can thus be applied in a quite novel way.

The way the components of a situation interact is summarized in the table on page 97.

4. Method (How?)

Explicit recommendations about the way language might actually be taught are well beyond the scope of this document. *Waystage* and *Threshold Level* specifications are sufficiently flexible to allow for the development of many parallel and radically different frameworks and methods. However, there are in the specifications implications which will apply to all kinds of language courses, however diverse the approaches may be. All courses based on functional/notional models must take as their starting point that communication must be taught and is therefore the primary objective, not merely the by-product of other objectives. It is worth considering briefly some of the problems which course designers who are attempting to implement functional/notional principles are likely to have in common. These will include:

Lesson organization
Transfer
Presentation
The teaching of grammar
Receptive and productive skills
Correctness
Testing

4.1 Lesson organization

The structural/lexical syllabus has as its ultimate aim the acquisition of a grammatical system together with a serviceable vocabulary. The structural grading sequence itself dictates the *pace* at which the student will proceed: the course designer is free to

The situational application of a functional approach to language teaching: summary

General functional categories	*Notions: General and specific*	*Settings and topics*	*Social, sexual and psychological roles*	*Style and range**	*Grammar and lexis*
Language acts operating through	*What?*	*Where?*	*Who?*	*How?*	*With what means?*
1. Factual 2. Intellectual 3. Emotional 4. Moral 5. Suasive 6. Social Two types of exponents: 1. Fixed phrases 2. 'Grammatical system'	Often abstract: appropriate to a large variety of topics and situations Directly determined by the choice of topic	Concrete→ transaction General→ open-ended conversation or argument	Friends Strangers Officials etc.	Style: formal informal Range: 'cline': certain tentative uncertain	As they arise in each situation

Examples:

1. Inquiring about Are there	the availability of tickets any tickets for tonight's performance?	Concrete: box office	Stranger/ Official	Formal	As in example
2. Inquiring about Are there	the existence of theatres any good theatres in your area?	General	Friend/ Friend	—	As in example

*Less applicable at *Waystage*.

97

speed up or slow down the build-up of structures in accordance with the type of learner he is addressing. Alternative forms of organization, through the application of *Waystage* and *Threshold Level* specifications, will greatly alter this fairly straightforward approach to pacing. Any consideration of pacing is likely to bring with it the need to consider the possibility of individualized study to enable learners to proceed at varying speeds. Some kind of route planning may have to be developed which allows the false beginner to skip certain exercises, while at the same time providing the slow learner with additional material.

4.2 Transfer

This can be defined as the ability to use language acquired in the classroom to meet actual needs in real life situations. It is singly the most important factor in the language learning process, for the learner's success is measured according to the extent he can use language in actual situations. As the emphasis in these specifications is on *communication*, it follows that transfer (often ignored in the structurally-based course) will be a key factor in course design. Transfer can take two basic forms: *actual* and *simulated*.

4.2.1 Actual transfer

Questions can be directed at the learner which relate to his own experiences. For example, if the subject of a dialogue is a visit to a cinema, the learner might be asked when he last visited a cinema, how much he paid for his seat, who he went with, where he sat, what he saw, how he enjoyed the film, and so on. This *actual transfer* is because the student is responding truthfully in a conversational context. This kind of transfer carries with it the possibility of student-imposed language: the student should be able to add items as and when he needs them. *Waystage* makes provision for this possibility by allowing a certain amount of open-endedness with regard to vocabulary. Certain items underscored + + + + + + are to be regarded as open-ended. Thus, if the topic of the lesson is jobs and the student wants to say what he actually does for a living, he can ask the teacher for the appropriate English word(s).

4.2.2 Simulated transfer

This involves role playing and improvising in particular situations so that patterns learnt in one context are re-combined to serve the exigencies of another. (The *common core* principle described in the *Waystage* introduction allows for precisely this kind of possibility.) A student may be asked to pretend that he is in a particular situation and he has to respond accordingly. He may be required to act in his own persona or in the persona of someone else. For example, we may set up a situation in which Student A (acting in his own persona) is buying a pair of shoes from Student B (acting in the persona of a shop assistant) and is inquiring about size, price, colour, suitability and so on. Again there is scope for student-imposed language. Such a simulated situation can occur very early in a course so it follows that a good deal of scene setting will be in the student's own language.

4.2.3 Presentation

It is reasonable to ask how a functional/notional approach will affect the audio-visual methodology commonly used in structurally-based beginners' courses. Audio-visual

98

methodology has the great advantage of enabling teachers and students to operate monolingually for the most part right from the beginning of a course. At a later stage there may be a transition to audio-lingual presentation when students become less dependent on pictures to understand meaning and more dependent on language itself. There is no reason why this principle should not continue in functionally-based courses. It will still be possible to present situations audio-visually or audio-lingually according to level. However, as has already been noted (4.2.2) role playing activities will require the use of the students' own language in the classroom for scene-setting purposes. This means that multi-lingual classes will become more difficult to conduct. Only different language-editions of a particular course (in which rubrics are in the students' own language) may get round this problem.

4.4 The teaching of grammar

When using structurally-based courses, teachers generally debate whether they should drill new language patterns before presenting a situation or after presenting one. This does not alter the fact that patterns are acquired for their own sake, since the ultimate objective of the course is the acquisition of the grammatical system. As we have seen, in *Waystage* and *Threshold Level* specifications this is only part of the objective. It follows that we do not need to acquire grammatical patterns unless we intend to put them to immediate use. This may well be the criterion for selecting grammatical items and practising them in functionally-based material. We must therefore think of grammar teaching within the context of communication. From 'grammar' to 'communication' might be seen as a three-part activity:

Practice ———▶ Practice context ———▶ Role playing/improvisation

4.4.1 Practice

Practice may involve the acquisition of a paradigm which has been isolated because of its relevance within a communicative framework. When practising *be* and verb forms, students have to learn how to (a) make affirmative statements; (b) make negative statements; and (c) handle question and answer forms. For example, paradigms involving the use of *there is* may be practised in this way. (*There is . . . There isn't . . . Is there . . .?*)

4.4.2 Practice context

Once the student has understood and become fluent in using a particular form, he can practise it within a context. To pursue the example of *There is* given in 4.4.1, the student might be presented with a tourist map in which certain buildings are indicated and controlled exchanges may be based on this context (eg *Is there a bank near here? Yes, there's one in West Street*). The raw structure previously acquired is now being put to use in a controlled way.

4.4.3 Role playing/improvisation

The final phase is to get the student to role play and improvise a situation which (a) makes use of the structure that has just been acquired and (b) enables the student to use functions and structures he has previously learnt. A situation involving eg actual

99

street maps would enable students to put the *There is* structure already practised (*see* 4.4.1 and 4.4.2) to further (simulated) use in suitably devised situations.

4.5 Receptive and productive skills

In *Waystage* no attempt is made to indicate the extent of the student's receptive command of the language, though this is attempted at *Threshold Level* in which receptive items are marked 'R'. It is clear that while the learner may control what he wishes to say, he can never have any control over the language other people will use. This means that he will have to be trained to understand the gist of what people are saying even at the earliest stages of learning and this is recognized in these specifications. This implies that the student may have to be trained to 'get the gist' by being presented with materials which are beyond his productive command. Such materials may be devised by the course designer or taken from authentic sources.

4.6 Correctness

The paramount aim in a communicative course is to enable students to communicate effectively. In traditional courses correctness is sometimes over-emphasized to the extent that errors in pronunciation and/or grammar are often considered a serious matter whether they interfere with communication or not. Using a language may be considered to be a performing skill: as with any other skill, performing ability will vary greatly from individual to individual. It may be a waste of time to demand near-native perfection from performers who will never be able to provide it. Our aim should be to ensure that the misuse of language is not so serious as to obscure communicative intentions. While we must always draw the line at wholly unacceptable utterances, the degree of error we are prepared to tolerate is bound to vary in accordance with the abilities of individual learners. 'Defective but effective communication' may be a reasonable aim if it means our students are not to be discouraged and defeated by the demands of perfection.

4.7 Testing

Waystage and *Threshold Level* specifications can be manipulated to yield criteria for testing. Ideally, testing objectives should be the same as teaching objectives, so there is no conflict between the two activities. Much of the language testing that is conducted in relation to structurally-based courses tends to divide language up into separate compartments from 'sound discrimination' to 'multiple choice comprehension' and this carries with it the implication that language should be taught in this way. But what has been conveniently evolved for rapid objective marking may not be the ideal tool from a teaching point of view. It is possible that entirely new kinds of tests will have to be developed to accompany functionally-based courses, for we are ultimately concerned not with how much the student knows, but how well he performs. Techniques used for teaching may then be very similar to those used for testing. The possibility that continual assessment (to include self-assessment) should be a standard part of course design is something to be considered.

4.8 Conclusion

Perhaps in the past we over-simplified the business of language learning/teaching and were not particularly intimidated by it. If in the present we are swinging the other way, it is right we should be intimidated and possibly rise to the challenge. Documents like *Waystage* and the *Threshold Level* are intended to be helpful tools for our use. At the same time we should be wary of attaching to them any mystique or regarding them as sacrosanct. Though language may be conveniently codified for reference purposes, it retains that resilient flexibility that made it language in the first place. And this is something we should never lose sight of.